bamboo

swaying

in the

wind

Father George Bernard Wong, S.J., 1999.

bamboo

swaying

in the

wind

A SURVIVOR'S STORY OF

FAITH AND IMPRISONMENT

IN COMMUNIST CHINA

Claudia Devaux and George Bernard Wong, S.J.

LOYOLAPRESS.

CHICAGO

LOYOLAPRESS.

3441 N. ASHLAND AVENUE
CHICAGO, ILLINOIS 60657

Interior design by Amy Evans McClure

Library of Congress Cataloging-in-Publication Data

Devaux, Claudia, 1946–
    Bamboo swaying in the wind : a survivor's story of faith and imprisonment in
  Communist China / Claudia Devaux and George Bernard Wong.
       p. cm.
    Includes bibliographical references.
    ISBN 0-8294-1458-4
    1. Wong, George Bernard, 1918– 2. Jesuits—China—Biography. I. Title: Survivor's
  story of faith and imprisonment in Communist China. II. Wong, George Bernard,
  1918– III. Title.

BX3743.W66 D49 2000
272'.9'092—dc21
[B]
                                                                    00-027371
                                                                          CIP

Printed in the United States of America
00 01 02 03 / 10 9 8 7 6 5 4 3 2 1

DEDICATED TO THE MEMORY OF

✥

Father Francis A. Rouleau, S.J. (1900–1984),
who inspired his young Chinese friend to follow the gleam,

✥

Sister Candida (Gladys) Wei, S.S.S. (1910–1981),
whose friendship nourished the vocation of the Jesuit priest,

✥

Father Peter Joseph Fleming, S.J. (1939–1994),
whose research on the Jesuit missionaries in China
permeates the commentary on the following pages, and

✥

Father Edward J. Malatesta, S.J. (1932–1998),
for whom bamboo swaying in the wind
represented a glimpse of the Chinese-Christian encounter
already here and still to come.

⁜ table of contents ⁜

⁂ foreword ⁂

It is a privilege to introduce this book about a remarkable fellow Jesuit—Chinese in origin and Californian by adoption—whose personal conversion to faith in Christ sustained him through lengthy imprisonment under Chinese Communism. Claudia Devaux has done a superb job of reading her way into a vast literature as context for her carefully transcribed account of a twentieth-century tale with important East-West implications for the Catholic Church of our time.

The late Edward Malatesta, S.J., founder of the University of San Francisco's Ricci Institute for Chinese-Western Cultural History, stated that this was "the first extensive study of a noteworthy Chinese Jesuit who has lived in the twentieth century; it is the first work to attend to the cross-cultural influences in the life of a Chinese Jesuit…of traditional Chinese culture and the ideals and customs of an Order founded by a sixteenth-century nobleman and soldier turned religious reformer," St. Ignatius of Loyola.[1]

Many others, including some of his Jesuit brothers, have tried unsuccessfully to access the personal story of Father George Bernard

Wong, S.J. It was too daunting a task for Father Wong to engage in seeming interrogations reminiscent of the prison experience that he was wanting to leave behind. In a combination of seaside vacationing and relaxed conversation, Ms. Devaux coaxed this narrative from Father Wong's blocked memory.

Ms. Devaux tells Father Wong's story in first person, preceded, in each chapter, by introductory notes that provide supplementary information and set a broader cultural context for the narrative. General readers, as well as the Catholic Church in particular, stand to benefit from this inspirational account of how Father Wong bridged East and West in living his Jesuit vocation at the service of Chinese Christianity in this time.

All of us who have been touched by Father Wong's gentle person and moving story are challenged in our own sense of what Christian discipleship and the missionary spirit mean in terms of dedication, openness, and inculturation as the Catholic Church moves through its post–Vatican II transition into dialogue with the contemporary world.

Paul J. Bernadicou, S.J.
Chair, Theology Department
University of San Francisco
Summer 1999

✤ prologue ✤

They came for me at eleven o'clock the night of September 26th, 1955. "Get up!" they ordered.

A rented car took me to Railway Station Jail where political prisoners were held in custody. Wardens searched my person and inspected the partial dentures I had even then. They took my watch, my rosary, and my scapular medal. I had to sign an acknowledgment of my arrest and then, before midnight, I was assigned to a small cell on the third floor.

Even though there was only one wooden plank on the floor, I shared the cell with another prisoner, a telegraph operator, who was perhaps in his late twenties or early thirties. We were not supposed to talk. As I wondered how we would sleep on the single wooden plank, I realized that I had forgotten to bring the bundle I had prepared.

There was a knock on the door, and I heard my name: One Three Two Seven. For the next seven years, that is, between 1955 and 1962, I would be addressed as One Three Two Seven. I was summoned to a small room where a large sign proclaimed, "Leniency to those who

confess, severity to those who hide." When I saw the four interrogators, I was reminded of my philosophy and theology exams; there
were always four examiners, and they couldn't all ask questions at
the same time.

The interrogation continued from half past midnight until half
past one the next afternoon. At about six in the morning, I had a hard
time not dozing off. They wanted to know all about my life, all my
acquaintances, all my connections. They repeated, "Don't be afraid
to confess. The more you confess the better. Don't try to hide anything." A written deposition covering my life, my work, and my relations was required.

Even though I knew that death was always a possible outcome and
remembered vividly the example of the first Chinese Jesuit to die in
prison at the hands of the Communists, Father Beda Tsang, I was not
afraid; rather I was bolstered by his example. Moreover, I remembered Jesus' telling his disciples not to worry about being called
before judges and magistrates as the Holy Spirit would furnish the
words. I might have interpreted this passage as saying that, thanks to
the Holy Spirit, eloquent speech would flow from the mouth, but
that is not exactly the way it worked. I took comfort in John Henry
Newman's saying not to worry about what you say as working against
you because, in one way or another, it will eventually work in the
Lord's favor.

St. Paul also said that all things work together for good for those
who love the Lord, so I did not agonize over my situation. Without
searching for answers or probing for understanding, I simply knew,
and deeply so, that I trusted God.

—*from chapter 10, "Before Magistrates and Judges"*

❖ 1 ❖

Baby of Borden

AMERICANS JOINED EUROPEANS *in creating spheres of influence in China when, in spite of opposition to foreign trade by the Ch'ing dynasty, a series of wars in the nineteenth century forced the country to open up. Thanks largely to the work of Chinese laborers, America had seen the joining of its eastern and western shores with the completion of the Transcontinental Railroad in 1869.*

This linking of East and West would continue across the "Ocean of Great Peace," where three groups—merchants, missionaries, and diplomats—were struggling to bring what they perceived as the blessings of the heavenly kingdom and the blessings of democracy and capitalism to the Republic of China, a nation born in 1911 after more than two thousand years of imperial dynastic rule. Of the three groups of Americans, only the missionaries had prolonged contact with the Chinese.

George Wong was born in 1918 in the Portuguese province of Macao, a port west of the mouth of the Zhu Jian (Pearl River) estuary in China. That same year, World War I fighting ceased with the surrender of Germany. The year before Wong's birth, Peking had joined the Allies. The year after, at the peace conference in Versailles, the Chinese request to end foreign concessions in China was ignored; the Allies sacrificed China in order to entice Japan to join the League of Nations.

This was a humiliating betrayal to the Chinese and a death blow to democracy in China. In 1921, the Chinese Communist Party was formed; an antiforeign and anti-Christian campaign would continue throughout the 1920s. Hua Quan, the Little Flower who was to become George Wong, was nourished on imported milk. After his birth, his father's business declined.

✢   ✢   ✢

MY FATHER WORKED on board ship as a compradore, or business agent for English-speaking foreigners. He had eight children in all; four were my half brothers and half sister of whom I met only one, my father's eldest. I was about thirteen and she was in her thirties when I visited with her and her husband, a Chinese who had studied in San Francisco, returning to China with a huge 1907 edition of *Webster's International Dictionary,* which he bequeathed to me. But I am getting ahead of my story.

When this sister's mother, my father's first wife, died, he married again. There were other children, including a half brother, my Fifth Brother, who died in his adolescence near my cot when I was a baby. My father always had a wife with him. Number One died. Then came Number Two wife. She also died, from what I heard. Then another one. Even without his wife's death, Father would get another one, a practice that was not unusual during the Ch'ing Dynasty. And so my mother was Number Four.

Mother lived in Shanghai; my father's house was in Macao. I don't have any idea as to how my parents met but imagine that it was through friends. As a traveling merchant, Father rode on a coastal steamer from Macao to Hong Kong to Shanghai, and then from Shanghai to Hong Kong, back to Macao.

My earliest childhood recollection is of being in my father's home in Macao, where *Sei-ga-je*—that is, my Fourth Sister, who would later be called Alice—cared for me and my brother, Willie. Born on the twenty-ninth day of the eleventh lunar month of the Year of the Snake—that is, on January 11, 1918, on the solar calendar—I was the youngest of all the children. My Chinese name was *Huang Hua Quan*. *Huang* would eventually become Wong, and my first name would be George; *Hua Quan*, meaning Little Flower, was rarely used, for in my early childhood my sister Alice called me *Ah-Sai*, or Little One.

Alice was eighteen years my senior. Rosie, known to me as *Lu-ga-je*, or Sixth Sister, was about twelve years older than I. Shortly after I was born, for reasons I can't explain, Mother returned to Shanghai with Rosie. During those early years I met Rosie only once in Macao when she came to visit for the Chinese New Year celebration; it was the Year of the Rooster, and she arrived at the house in a rickshaw, waving a toy rooster with shiny brown and black feathers she had brought me as a gift. My brother, Willie, *Chat-goh,* or Elder Seventh Brother, was three at the time of my birth.

And so Alice, Willie, and I lived together in Father's house in Macao. Alice was my nurse, and she nurtured me on imported Borden's milk, obtained easily enough by my father from the ship's purveyor. Fourth Sister, that is, Alice, told me that when Seventh Brother, Willie, was born, my father's business prospered, or in her words, it rose to high tide. But when I came, Father's business sank to low tide.

Fourth Sister loved us, me especially, for I was the Benjamin of the family, the youngest. She was good to us, although our pranks sometimes merited scoldings. I remember her chasing my brother with a feather duster, but she never spanked me. There was the time I pushed a table next to the cupboard on top of which Alice had placed a tin of cookies out of my reach. I put a stool on the table and then climbed first onto the table and then onto the stool only to fall to the floor, biting my lip in the fall. I still have the scar. Fourth Sister didn't know whether to scold me or comfort me. She gave me a hug.

We lived on the second floor in the house in Macao. A large room faced the street, and there were two smaller rooms for sleeping. In the living room was a long ebony table of medium width on a low platform alongside the wall. A couple of idols sat on the table next to joss sticks on an earthen burner and red candles that were lit on occasion. On the wall hung calligraphic scrolls. The stairway was long with wide steps but insufficient lighting; I tripped myself on it more than once, rolling sideways all the way down to the ground floor.

There were no rooms on the ground floor, but near the bottom of the stairs was a huge well, our source of water. Having heard stories about people drowning, I steered clear of it except in the company of my brother. We did not have electricity but used oil lamps, and yet I remember striking the electric wires strung outside the second-floor back bedroom window with a bamboo pole. I stopped this amusement when cautioned about a short circuit even though I did not know what a short circuit was. During downpours we had to close the windows facing the street lest the rainwater splash into the room, making it hot and muggy. Wondering where the rain came from, I remember spotting an old-fashioned biplane upon opening the window after a shower. My conclusion was that the plane brought the rain.

There were daily goings-on in the street outside our house. Every morning at seven o'clock we could buy bread loaves and buns from an itinerant baker who was quite distinguished in having a large goiter under his chin that looked like one of the buns he was peddling. We called him *meen bao loh,* or bread man, with no disparagement to his goiter. Also available was a portable street kitchen that catered to a taste for *yu sang ju yuk jook,* or congee with raw fish slices and meatballs. In the afternoon, there were vendors of sweet sesame-seed paste and red-bean congee; they peddled ice cream in the summer as well.

Sometimes a peanut vendor would sell his roasted peanuts and a song on the fiddle. You could drop your coins from the window for a packet of peanuts, which he would toss up from the street below. Other delicacies were better hauled up in a basket tied to a string. On certain occasions there was a monkey show; a crowd would gather and the monkey would mimic people to the accompaniment of a little gong or small cymbals. At night, after people had stopped playing mahjong, they could purchase dumplings and noodles from a portable street kitchen as the vendor struck his Chinese castanets. We rarely had visitors playing mahjong so late, but when we did, my sister would wake me to share in the dumplings.

From the window we watched funeral processions; the mourners, wearing coarse white hemp, were accompanied by a brass band playing some Western-style dirge. They would be followed by a line of horse-drawn carriages transporting relatives and friends of the deceased to the place of interment, which was not necessarily the cemetery; sometimes it was a solitary mound in the countryside. And there were wedding parades too, with the bride being carried in a decorated sedan while sprightly music, like "Johnny, Get Your Gun, Get Your Gun" from World War I, was played. More exciting and distinguished were the parades of certain business enterprises that showed off their success in celebrating their anniversaries. There were flags and banners along the route and exploding firecrackers and bands playing both Western and Oriental music.

During my early childhood, I was well acquainted with my father, who came home at intervals during his intermittent voyages from Macao to Shanghai and back. He was affable, and I can vividly recall one afternoon sitting on his feet, placed together at the insteps, enjoying so much the horseback-like heaving up and down. When he had to stop playing in order to attend to some business away from home, I felt so disappointed and frustrated that I cried inconsolably.

When he returned home, he brought with him some delicacy to make up for my crying.

I got along very well with *Chat-goh,* or Elder Seventh Brother, following him wherever he went to play. Once we joined the neighborhood boys in sliding down an inclined cobblestone street on a board that had been soaped on the underside to make it slippery. It happened that a Portuguese policeman making the beat on an upper street did not permit our playing with the skidding board, but we continued just the same. The policeman then came to chastise us, punching each boy on the chest. My brother and I, the last targets of the cop, were lucky. Willie got only a light tap on the ribs, and I, the smallest of the group, was spared. The incident was a kind of omen of the leniency I would be accorded for my weakness among others who were bigger or stronger.

George Wong and his brother, Willie, 1925.

Father Wong's father, Francis Wong, 1930.

Family portrait, 1938. Alice, Willie, Mother, George, and Rosie Wong.

George Wong on his first day in the United States, 1939.

George Wong with the Edward Rouleau family: "Uncle Ed," Jacqueline, Darrell, Marilyn ("Missy"), "Aunt Mabel," and Joan (to become Sister Mary Celeste, R.S.M.). Los Gatos, California, 1940.

✣ 2 ✣

A Confucian Scholar

A BUDDHIST CEREMONY *marked the initiation of the child as a scholar following a tradition, axiological and academic, that had endured for over two thousand years. Confucius (551–479 B.C.) developed a code of morals based on relationships of individuals so that people could live together in harmony. Mencius (371–ca. 288 B.C.), referred to as the second sage, emphasized the innate goodness of humans, family duty as the foundation of society, and the need for rulers to be concerned about the common people—all of which played a major role in the development of Confucianism.*

Italian Jesuit missionary Matteo Ricci (1552–1610) introduced Confucianism to Europe in the form of a dialogue between two friends, an Eastern scholar and a Western scholar. Ricci's work greatly contributed to Enlightenment thinking, which, ironically, engendered the dualism that places science and rational thought in opposition to religion and theology. Ricci, however, engaged in a systematic study of Confucianism that led him to passages reflecting the Christian faith on matters such as the unity of God, the immortality of the soul, and the glory of the blessed. He preached the gospel from a Chinese perspective, interpreting the Chinese name T'ien (Heaven) as God and concluding that ancestral ceremonies on the part of Chinese converts were not in conflict with their Christian faith.

A decree from Pope Alexander VII in 1656 approved the proposal of Ricci's Jesuit successors regarding tolerance of the ceremonies honoring the deceased as long as they did not involve superstitious activities. However, not all missionaries were in agreement. Their protests gave way to what would be called the Chinese Rites Controversy. In 1742, a papal bull signed by Benedict XIV forbade the Rites, required an oath of silence with regard to further debate on the subject, and made a point of addressing the Jesuits in particular.

For the Chinese, ambiguity was a way of life. The elder Wong did not find it necessary to choose between Buddhism, whose adherents strive to rid themselves of attachments because they lead to suffering, and Confucianism, a set of codes designed to maintain harmony by conserving the social order. And yet Wong did not see his sons' future in the old social order. Himself in daily contact with foreign merchants and certainly aware of the weakness of the new republican government, Wong, now the pragmatic Taoist moving with the flow, consented to a Western education for the boys.

❖   ❖   ❖

WE WERE BUDDHISTS. My sisters were educated Chinese-style at home. My father was well-to-do then, so private tutors came to the house. My own formal education started in a school setting when I was five years of age, that is, five years of age Chinese style. The Chinese count birth from conception, so I was only four years old by Western standards when my father invited a couple of bonzes—Buddhist priests—to our house to officiate at a ceremony commemorating my birthday and the beginning of my education. I was dressed like a little gentleman in a black silk jacket and a red skull cap with a red pom-pom. The bonzes, wearing their ceremonial robes, burned incense and offered cups of wine and other food to the god of wisdom, seeking his blessing for me to become a good scholar. Along with the others present, I had my turn to kowtow to the god of wisdom as bells tinkled and sutras were chanted. We had a hearty meal afterward.

Joining my brother at school, I learned the teachings of Mencius, the Confucian philosopher who lived three centuries before Christ. My first calligraphy lesson, with the radical strokes for the meaning and then other strokes for the sound, involved tracing with a Chinese pen: *"Yen zi zot zi boon san,"* Cantonese for "Man, at the beginning, seeks goodness." Calligraphy lessons continued, with the sound more predominant in my child's mind than the meaning.

Although just a little boy, I was very particular about my clothes and was especially fond of a red-striped cotton coat and matching trousers because they looked like the American flag. I recall that one morning before going to school I had to wait for my sister to finish sewing the buttons on my new, swanky outfit. A few months after I started school, my mother came to take me away.

My sister and brother spoke of her as Mother, but to others, and to me, she was *Sei-nai,* or Fourth Lady. One day as she was washing clothes in a tub, she beckoned me. "Ah-Sai, Little One, come here. Do not call me Fourth Lady," she instructed. "You are to call me Mama." Mama, with the accent on the second syllable. She and my aunt, her sister, would be taking my brother and me to Shanghai for a Western education.

Her sister was not really her sister. A servant in the family, she was eventually adopted—this kind of arrangement was not unusual in Chinese households—and she made a good marriage to a British subject. Even my own maternal grandfather was English; Rudland was his name. I never knew him but understood that he was quite wealthy, having two mansions. My mother, as was the custom, was family trained. She could not read or write, but she knew how to manage a house and to cook. My mother's mother, whom I didn't know either, had left two thousand taels, or Chinese dollars, of higher value than the ordinary yuan, for the education of my brother and me.

Going to Shanghai was one thing; leaving Fourth Sister was another. I clung to her. Calling me by my baby name, Ah-Sai, she asked, "Would you like some litchi?" Litchi is a very sweet, watery fruit with a shell. Of course, I was willing to let go of her so that she could fetch the litchi. She sneaked away, and I was brought to the boat. That was the last I saw of her for seven years. At first I was disappointed, wondering where my litchi was and where my sister was, but looking back, I respected her for her cleverness. She was really acting in my best interest.

When I saw her again seven years later, my affection was not as fervent as that of a five-year-old; that was something of a defect on my part. I knew that she loved me, but as a twelve-year-old I was annoyed by her constantly telling everyone how much she loved me and how good I was. Her affection was too sugary for a boy my age, but her ruse had gained my respect.

Anyway, here were my mother, aunt, brother, and I on board a steamer bound for Shanghai. The voyage should have taken five days, including a short visit to some relatives in Hong Kong, but our trip took ten because the ship was attacked by pirates outside Bias Bay. They damaged the engine and chopped off a leg of the foreign captain while he was in bed.

Word spread on board ship that the pirates were stealing valuables. One elderly lady was said to have concealed some bank notes in her trousers, but they were found and seized. My mother and aunt had hidden the two thousand dollars that was to cover the tuition of my brother and me inside a second row of clay jars stored beneath our bunk. The pirates checked the first row of jars, which were empty except for some cooking utensils; they didn't bother to check the second row. They did take jewelry from my mother and aunt, and they got my aunt's rosary. A Catholic, she had given me the silver rosary to play with, hoping that the pirates would overlook a plaything. However, noticing that it was silver, they snatched it.

What concerned my mother and my aunt the most was that they might kidnap my brother and me for ransom. They wore masks made from handkerchiefs, with holes for their eyes. Frightened by all this wicked commotion, I began to cry, and one of the pirates shouted an order to the cabin boy. "Boy, get some hot water and make some tea for this kid who's crying!" I was given something piping hot to eat. It came straight from the oven, and I had to eat slowly.

We eventually arrived in Shanghai where, at first, we lived with my aunt and her husband, whose last name was Randle. A British subject, he was a Protestant and a Mason who was tolerant with regard to his wife's Catholic faith. He made a special shelf for the placement of my aunt's statues of the Holy Family: the Blessed Mother, the Sacred Heart, and St. Joseph. This uncle was the one who gave my sisters and brother and me our Western names—Alice, Rosie, Willie, and George—which became our baptismal names.

The uncle was kindhearted. He used to go to his club for foreigners every week to visit with his buddies, returning always with a dime for us children. A good deal older than my aunt, he was her legal husband, but she also had another, younger husband who, like her, was Catholic and who brought some additional income to the household. Well, that was her business; the arrangement was not an issue.

❖ 3 ❖

Orphans at School

*D*EEP AND LASTING *friendships developed between sixteenth- and seventeenth-century Jesuit missionaries and Chinese scholars. Matteo Ricci, appointed in 1597 as superior of the Jesuits working in China, came to listen, learn, and share his knowledge and his faith. Fluent in Chinese and well versed in the classics, he engaged his friends in a dialogue on science, religion, music, and the arts. In contrast, the twentieth-century missionaries who operated schools such as the one young George Wong attended, however sincere and fervent, had come to China more to teach than to learn.*

Foreign missionaries—Protestant and Catholic—built schools, orphanages, and hospitals in China. Some brought science and technology to cities, and others, with no training in Chinese and very little knowledge of first aid, operated makeshift clinics in rural areas. They were advocates of public service and the abolition of prearranged marriages. More than any other group of foreigners, missionaries brought China into the modern world, and yet they were considered by some a nuisance to social order; even the good they brought about implied change.

Perceiving themselves as China's greatest friends, missionaries set themselves apart from merchants, diplomats, and soldiers. But they sought privileges and the protection of treaties, sometimes taking foolish risks only to expect a diplomatic or military bailout. Though generally sincere in their desire to spread the gospel, missionaries could be arrogant, insensitive, and patronizing. Some Chinese families operated their own schools; other Chinese families saw in the mission schools the opportunity for their children to acquire the language, skills, and certificates that would gain them access to jobs and professions in a world governed by foreign economics.

George Wong attended St. Francis Xavier College, founded in 1874 by Jesuits and, due to a lack of personnel, handed over to French Marists in 1896. The school had a section for Chinese nationals and an international section that prepared foreign boys for the Cambridge Overseas Examination. Coming from Macao, little Hua Quan spoke Cantonese, not the Shanghai dialect, at the time of his enrollment; he was placed in the international section where lessons were conducted in English.

❖ ❖ ❖

IN SHANGHAI, THERE was a British-dominated international settlement, and the French had their own concession. My aunt had many foreign connections; among them was the Jesuit pastor of Sacred Heart Church in Shanghai. He introduced us to the brother director of the school run by the French Marists, St. Francis Xavier College, which was within the parish boundaries. The school had both primary and secondary sections, and followed a curriculum to prepare boys for the Cambridge Overseas Exams.

My mother offered the brothers the two thousand dollars for our tuition, and they accepted Willie and me as boarders for the duration of our scholarity. There were two categories of boarders: those who could pay for the extras, like butter at meals, and those who got by with the essentials, like sardines on Friday. The latter group were more or less charity pupils known as "orphans." My brother and I, though our parents were living, were among the orphans. There was no great hardship in being a so-called orphan, but to this day I have an aversion to sardines.

I was at St. Francis Xavier College for the next ten years. For the last year, the brothers transferred me into the group enjoying the better food and better treatment. Also, a prosperous alumnus set up a scholarship for deserving scholars, and on Christmas of my final year, I was awarded, out of the blue, a hundred dollars.

Our lessons were in English, although we learned French as well. Discipline was strict, but the brothers really were kind at heart. Once I was punished for talking in a frivolous manner. I had to stand by a column in the corner for one or two hours, but I could read. Punishments could be in the form of writing lines over and over or copying and memorizing text from the English dictionary. These were useful punishments.

Since this was a religious school, we had catechism and Mass every day. Even though at the beginning I was not Catholic, I did not mind going to Mass. Kneeling on our seats—our desks had a table and a seat—we said the rosary at noon and a Hail Mary every hour. The brothers wanted us to be not just good Catholics but fervent Catholics. With my parents' approval, my brother and I were baptized. I was about seven or eight, and my Buddhist mother encouraged me in my prayers. "You know," she told me, "you can pray while you are walking."

During my first years in Shanghai, my mother did not live in her own house. Rosie lived with my aunt while Alice remained in Macao. After Sunday Mass, my brother and I left our boarding school to have the midday meal with my aunt and other relatives, some of whom had Eurasian backgrounds. The midday meal was Western style with knives and forks, and the evening meal was Chinese style with chopsticks. The aunt and her friends spoke Cantonese. The adults were interested in us, so it wasn't so much a matter of propriety that kept us from lengthy conversations; we just didn't have that much to share. The adults played mahjong while my brother and I enjoyed the company of our cousins, boys and girls, all of whom were in Western schools. We were more at ease with English than Cantonese.

Because my mother had a job taking care of an American baby, she lived with that family. We were not sleeping under the same roof, yet our family ties were strong, and my parents had a good marriage that I think was largely the outcome of my mother's loyalty. When my father was forced to retire because he fell on board ship and injured his ankle, he came to Shanghai. Then the six of us—two parents, two sisters, and two brothers—lived together in the same house, although Willie and I remained as boarders at school for the duration of our studies, coming home for holidays.

I remember being at home once when I was about twelve. I had an ache in my stomach. My mother heated salt in a pan and then wrapped the hot salt pebbles in a cloth, which she placed on my abdomen. It was traditional Chinese medicine, and it worked.

My sisters started a business making and selling jam. They used to get orange peels from the kitchen of the Catholic hospital for marmalade. The two sisters had made a vow of virginity so that they could look after my brother and me. It might have appeared that Willie was the one destined for the priesthood; at school they called him Holy Man because he seemed to pray longer than most. But when Willie finished school, he moved home permanently, getting a job at an American bakery called Bake-Rite. Eventually he married Julie, a Protestant who became Catholic and moved into the house with Mother, Alice, and Rosie.

At age sixteen, I sat for the Cambridge Overseas Exams. At St. Francis Xavier College, our preparation for these exams included mastering one Shakespearean play a year. I remember doing *Twelfth Night, The Tempest,* and *As You Like It.* We studied the poetry of Tennyson and read Dickens; I was impressed by how Dickens was sympathetic to the poor, the so-called underclass. We did the Gospels and the Acts of the Apostles. I liked literature but I wasn't very good at mathematics.

The examination took place in the British Town Hall, and, besides English and mathematics, it included an obligatory section in French. If you failed in French, you failed the entire exam. The problem was that for the three days prior to the examinations, we had been celebrating the Diamond Jubilee, or sixtieth anniversary of St. Francis Xavier College. There were three glorious days of entertainment with plays performed by the boys, old and new. So on the first day of the Cambridge Overseas Exams, I was very tired, dozing off in the afternoon during the written examination in French. I thought for sure that I would not pass the exam, but somehow I was lucky.

❖ 4 ❖

A Dandy

*T*HE SHANGHAI GEORGE WONG *knew as a young man had a popula-tion of over three million Chinese and approximately sixty thousand foreigners. Foreign concessions—Chinese lands technically belonging to another country—had been instituted in the city following the Opium Wars of the nineteenth century; French Jesuits flew the tricolor over their establishments. There were twelve foreign chambers of com-merce representing business interests and twelve foreign courts exercising jurisdiction over their respective nationals. American marines, British soldiers, members of the Japanese Naval Landing Party, and members of the Shanghai Volunteer Corps offered protection to foreigners.*

Foreign control of the city was most evident in the Bund, where the headquarters of Jardine Matheson was located near banks, the Palace Hotel, and the North China Daily News, *a British paper. There were thirteen different foreign-language newspapers. Foreign architecture*

*lent prestige to the city. Even the streets had foreign names, like Avenue
Joffre and Broadway. Georgetown University operated an alumni association in Shanghai. Foreign golf courses did not admit Chinese. There
was very little contact between native Chinese and foreigners.*

*It is said that some Hollywood films were shown in Shanghai even
before being shown in the United States. Along with the symphony
orchestra concerts were horse races and dog races, nightclubs and
cabarets, casinos and massage parlors, opium dealing and ear-wax
extraction services. The city was not one of culture or religion or government as much as it was one of moneymaking, and yet for all its opu-
lence, there was extreme poverty. Rickshaw pullers, beggars, adult and
child prostitutes, dying infants and old people were all part of the
Chinese population of Shanghai.*

*Shanghai was the birthplace of Confucius in 551 B.C., Mencius in
about 371 B.C., and the Chinese Communist Party in 1921. Following
the humiliation of the Treaty of Versailles in 1919, various groups
engaged in action against foreigners during the 1920s. By the 1930s all
missionary schools had to be registered, as did all foreign newspapers,
because of their criticism of the Chinese government.*

❖   ❖   ❖

ARMED WITH MY certificate from the Cambridge Overseas
Exams, I was able to get a job with a Chinese Catholic gentleman in Shanghai whose father, Sir Robert Hotung of Hong Kong,
had been knighted because of service he had rendered to the British
government. Sir Robert was not Catholic, but he sent his grandchildren to Catholic schools, and the son, Eddie Hotung, became
Catholic and married a woman from Ireland. I happened to know
Eddie and worked for him for six months.

Eventually, through newspaper advertisements, I found a job with
an Austrian firm that sold carbon paper. Things went along well for

one month, and then there was a telephone call in Chinese, Shanghai dialect, which I didn't understand. So I found myself jobless. Again, through the newspaper, I applied for a job, this time at Jardine Matheson and Company, a prestigious British import-export firm, and, probably because of the Cambridge Overseas Exams certificate, was selected from among two hundred applicants. I worked as a clerk for three years; my boss, a Portuguese Catholic, was a former St. Francis Xavier College boy, and we got along well.

During my post–secondary school days I found myself drawn to religious life and spiritual matters, and yet I was also very concerned about my appearance. In fact, while still in school, I hid in the lavatory during a photo session as I was too self-conscious to be in the school picture. As a young man and sort of a dandy, though still a teenager, I wanted my clothes to be impeccable and fashionable.

Although my reading included romanticized accounts of boyhood in America such as *The Adventures of Huckleberry Finn*, it was mostly serious. I did look forward to the monthly pamphlets of Father Daniel Lord that included music and entertainment and were very popular among young people. At the same time, I was absorbed in the lives of saints, not the opus by Butler but works by various other authors.

I also subscribed to *The Messenger of the Sacred Heart* from New York, having saved the money to do so. In those days, for any boy in China to subscribe to an American Catholic magazine was very rare. This magazine came every month, with beautiful art and fine articles on religious topics and questions of current interest such as divorce. I read each issue from cover to cover. I regularly read *America,* the magazine published by the American Jesuits, as well.

In its early times, there were some women writers, but then Father General Wlodimir Ledochowski said that only men should write for *America*, that women should write for women's magazines. Still, in the *America* of 1936, which appeared so modern and polished with double lines for captions and so forth, there were articles by women.

When the magazine was revamped, a friend of mine commented that it looked like a Communist publication. That was a compliment; the Communists are good at spectacular things. I followed the argument between *America* and *Commonweal* regarding the Spanish Civil War; *Commonweal,* begun by Michael Williams, a convert and a layman, was about the only lay-edited Catholic magazine then. Now there are more intellectuals among the laity.

I felt called to write my own responses to articles and to what I saw going on in my life. I saw my first sound movie in 1929; by the time I was in my final year of secondary school, that is, in 1934, there was a Legion of Decency in Shanghai. I had my own standards of decency. At sixteen, I thought that a film showing a shadowgraph of a man and woman on a bed was too suggestive, but, of course, that is nothing compared to now. At any rate, I wrote a letter to the editor of the English paper in Shanghai, stating my opinion on films that violated my standards of decency; I signed the letter Sixteen. One of the readers responded in the very popular correspondence column, referring to me as Sweet Sixteen.

Besides the opinions I submitted to the paper, I wrote an Easter article that appeared on the editorial page of a British journal. Inspired by Ronald Knox's modern English translation of the Bible, I wrote about the life of Christ before he was born, that is, on the prophecies of the Old Testament. But my article was centered on suffering, on the passion and death of Jesus according to the translation of Knox. I sent a copy to Knox, and he wrote back saying that he appreciated my article and my writing to him.

Later on, after the Communist takeover when I was a Jesuit, I sent a letter to the editor of the *China Daily* regarding the church. A Protestant friend, knowing that it would most likely not be published under my name, agreed to use his name and address. The letter was published, but only in the overseas edition to give the impression abroad that there was freedom of religion and freedom of speech in China. One of our fathers in Hong Kong happened to see the letter.

He commented to me, without knowing that I was the author, that it was well written and expressed some of his own thoughts.

After secondary school, I lived at home with my family. My brother had his job at the Bake-Rite bakery, my sisters conducted their marmalade business, and I was at Jardine Matheson and Company. We were a religious family. My father, as a Buddhist, kept his incense and candles on the windowsill and said his prayers daily, and yet he used to rouse my brother from his second-floor bedroom on Sunday morning for Mass. The ceiling downstairs was the floor upstairs, and my father would use a bamboo pole to tap on the ceiling to tell Willie to wake up. I also went to daily Mass; that is the way the Marists had brought me up.

My vocation began with a gentle light. I spoke to Brother Antony at St. Francis Xavier College about becoming a religious brother. When I entered the college, the top of my head barely reached the bottom of his beard. Now I towered over him. He gave me a book to read on the Marists. Because my education did not include Greek and Latin, I had not considered the priesthood.

Somehow, after attending daily Mass at Sacred Heart Church and finding the sermons particularly interesting and moving, I decided to contact a certain Father Tom Ryan, an Irish Jesuit whom I had actually met at a dinner party hosted by my former employer, Eddie Hotung, and his Irish wife. But when I went to see Father Ryan at the Sacred Heart rectory on July 27, 1937, he wasn't there, so I spoke briefly to a Father Francis Rouleau of the California Jesuits. Disappointed about missing Father Ryan, who had returned to Hong Kong, I looked at my wristwatch, later learning that Father Rouleau took that as a sign of my need to leave him. And so I left without fully realizing that Providence works in mysterious ways. That brief encounter with Father Rouleau would change my life.

❖ 5 ❖

Follow the Gleam

THE CALIFORNIA JESUITS, then still part of the U.S. Northwest Province that would be divided first in 1931 and again in 1932, had no desire to go to China; they had plenty of work to do, especially in the Alaskan and Indian missions. They were sent to China following the request of Chinese business magnate Lo Joseph Pahong to Pope Pius XI and Jesuit General Wlodimir Ledochowski. Lo Joseph Pahong wanted the American Jesuits to establish an English-speaking high school in Shanghai, but this particular goal was not communicated to the missionaries. Two priests and four scholastics (Jesuits still in the formation stage prior to ordination) arrived in 1928 with no significant preparation in terms of culture or language; they would find themselves under the direction of French superiors (French was the lingua franca of the Chinese and the foreigners in the Jesuit circle).

One of the California Jesuits, George H. Dunne, who found wanting the missions strategy of the early 1930s, had a vision for a new direction in the California Province Mission. He wanted to adapt Matteo Ricci's approach to modern China. Ricci and his contemporaries, in addressing the Mandarins, had focused on astronomy, cartography, and geography; Dunne urged studies in sociology, education, government, economics, literature, and agronomy for China's emerging young elite.

Whereas Lo Joseph Pahong wanted the Jesuits to teach English to Chinese students, Dunne wanted the Jesuits to master the Chinese language and to understand the culture in order to speak the gospel message from the Chinese perspective. In 1932, he predicted that unless something were done to develop a new breed of dynamic and democratic Chinese leaders who could replace the outworn economic, social, and political structures with new ones meaningful to the masses, China would fall into the hands of the Communists within thirty years. The Communist takeover happened seventeen years later, in 1949.

Francis A. Rouleau, another California Jesuit, arrived in Shanghai as a scholastic in 1929 and was ordained at the great Chinese cathedral at Zikawei in 1935. Like all other Catholic missionaries since 1742, he had taken an oath of silence regarding the Chinese Rites Controversy. Letters to home and articles written by Father Rouleau reflect his devotion to China, his love for the people, his passion for life, and his keen sense of humor.

In 1937, young George Wong encountered Father Rouleau just prior to the latter's departure for Nanking, where he would find himself helping refugees during the brutally devastating Japanese siege of the city. Upon returning to Shanghai, Father Rouleau became George Wong's spiritual father, calling him by his middle name, Bernard. Eighteen years older than George Wong, Father Rouleau was neither an authoritarian father substitute who would prescribe a set of steps to follow toward a specific goal nor the Zen master who would validate answers.

Rather he was a master who, Ignatian-like, would lead the young man to validate himself as he followed not a dream but a gleam. As guide and luminary model, Father Rouleau provided an encouraging presence without pushing, projecting, or imposing. By simply being himself, he presented a way of life that attracted the flow of the younger man's true nature from within himself.

❖   ❖   ❖

ALTHOUGH I HAD walked away from Father Rouleau that evening, I couldn't get him out of my mind. He had given me a warm welcome, and he struck me as being an uncommonly young-looking priest. Later I would find him so very dynamic and up to date. *Hu T'ien-lung,* or Dragon of Heaven, was his Chinese name, and it suited him. When word reached me that Father Rouleau had gone west to work at the Nanking Institute, I spontaneously wrote him a letter that was casual in tone but expressed my sincere hope that he would be safe. The Japanese military had begun menacing the Chinese capital, bombing the Nanking-Shanghai railway lines. Father Rouleau replied quickly and warmly, letting me know that he had made it safely to Nanking and explaining that he loved the Chinese people. Then I learned that he was back in Shanghai, recuperating at St. Joseph's Infirmary, a ten-minute walk from where I worked.

The Sino-Japanese War, as it is referred to now, began with the so-called China "Incident" on July 7, 1937, when the first shot was fired near Marco Polo Bridge in North China; this shot ignited a conflagration of war that was to continue for seven years. A few days later, cable wires buzzing, an initial home victory was celebrated in Shanghai with the jubilant ring of staccato firecrackers; but the successes were only temporary. Japan's war machine moved into the city, and, on the vigil of the Assumption at about ten o'clock in the morning, I saw the first bomb fall on Shanghai.

In Nanking, between August and October of 1937, Father Rouleau survived forty-nine aerial bombardments. The American consul and the Jesuit superior, Father Yves Henry, ordered him and his companion, Father James Kearney, to leave Nanking, something that disappointed him bitterly as they had joined with Protestants in helping the indigent Chinese after the bombings. Father Rouleau had just given his promise to remain in Nanking, and I know that he considered his leaving a loss of face.

Under orders, however, he hastily boarded a train that would be bombed by Japanese planes. The engineer, having spotted the approaching planes, did not slow down at Wuxi station but raced ahead in order to save the train from total destruction. When a bomb hit the third car, Father Rouleau, a second-class passenger in the fifth car, tucked up his soutane and hurled himself through the window, dropping to the cinder track below and taking refuge in a rice field.

Eventually arriving safely in Shanghai toward the end of 1937, Father found himself among priests and scholastics who had left the classrooms to help the crowds of refugees straggling into the Jesuit compound at Zikawei; Bishop Auguste Haouisée bade the missionaries to open their schools and their property to all. Aurora University received more than three thousand refugees, and two thousand crowded into the courtyard and playground at St. Ignatius College. There were farmers driven from their homes, village blacksmiths, carpenters, cobblers, shopkeepers, all sorts of artisans with their families. Father Rouleau recounted that the girls' orphanage alone was receiving an average of 160 babies a week.

Father Rouleau suffered from a heart condition that had kept him many years before from accepting an appointment at Annapolis, directing him instead to the California Jesuits. It now landed him in the infirmary for relief from the exhaustion of ministering to three thousand refugees. Though the infirmary was in a zone off limits to native Chinese without a special pass, I slipped in to visit wearing Western attire. Bringing my box lunch, I came often at noontime to see Father, happy to talk about many things on my mind, and some-times encountering Father's Jesuit confrères, who addressed him as Frank. With respect and familiarity, I then began calling him Father Frank; he called me Bernard.

At the end of 1937, Father Frank was still in the infirmary, and I was delighted to join the circle of friends gathered round to make sure that he had a good Christmas. On his birthday, January 23, he shared with us some fine fruitcake sent from Los Angeles by his sister Helen. During his convalescence, I brought a radio set so that Father Frank could listen to the *Shanghai Catholic Hour,* directed by Father Jack Lipman, another California Jesuit. By that time, Father Frank was able to sit up and walk a few steps around the room. At one point, I sent Father Frank a note in which I asked, "How beats your heart?" He responded in verse beginning with this preface:

> Wherein a Youth of old Cathay doth ask after the health of his dear friend, the Priest, and the latter doth respond accordingly from his sick bed, the whole being fashioned in meter of four feet.

I.

A young man asks God's anointed Priest,
    Who was stricken down at a gladsome feast
Of rice and clothing for his refugee flock—
    Gaunt and starving from warfare's shock.

Yes, broken was he in the blossom of life,
    While dreaming so fondly of chivalrous strife
For Christ his King and his Lady above,
    To whom he had vowed eternal love.

    How fares your heart?
    How fares your heart?

Glowing and fresh as an Autumn dawn,
    The lad's bright soul enquires anon;
Eager for a sign from the priestly hand
    That guided his youth toward the promised land.

His own heart kindles with the same emprise,
  To battle for Christ through joy and signs;
His chaste eyes cast on the Gleam afore,
  Enchanting his steps to an unknown shore.

  How beats your heart?
  How beats your heart?

II.

O youth of Sinim and brother of mine,
  Sealed by God with the coals divine;
Listen to the words I sing this night—
  Stretched on my back in helpless plight.

Steeled is my heart in the soldier's mould
  Of knightly Ignatius, the captain bold;
Aflame is my heart with apostle's grace
  For the cherished millions of this olden race.

  Thus fares my heart.
  Thus fares my heart.

O youthful dreamer, look up on high,
  At the Crucified Master against the sky;
Look at the purple breast heaving in pain,
  As the scourged Heart pulses its tortured refrain.

Ah, measure your beat on this Heart of love!
  Sorrow and tears as the Spring winds blow.
But laughter and life in that glorified place,
  Where two hearts pulse in a timeless embrace.

  Thus beats my heart.
  Thus beats my heart.

For three years since leaving St. Francis Xavier College, I had pondered and prayed about my vocation whose gentle light had grown more radiant. On January 28, 1938—I remember the date distinctly—I told Father Frank that I wanted, like him, to serve the church in China. But I was aware of certain obstacles. Although I had grown up in a family that spoke Cantonese, I had hardly any skill in reading and writing the characters of my native tongue. And although I was fluent in English and French, wasn't Latin required of those seeking ordination?

Father Frank encouraged me to follow the gleam, and after we had made a pact of loyalty to each other like Jonathan and David, he proposed a plan that at once allayed my fears and in time solved these problems. The first step, my having resolved to go onward, was to apply to the Jesuit Order in California; the Sacred Heart Novitiate in Los Gatos did not require a mastery of the Chinese language. When I had gone through the basics of Jesuit training in the United States, I should return to my homeland and, just as foreign missionaries do, undertake regular courses in Chinese. Before word of acceptance came from the California Provincial, Father Frank said that I would have plenty of time to make arrangements for departure from home and to study Latin and Chinese at Aurora University in Shanghai.

There was one other problem, that of my family. It wasn't just that my parents were Buddhists; there was the practical matter of the reduced household income with one son not working. Eventually I would quit my job at Jardine's, my elder brother, Willie, having agreed to support the family on his own, taking over my share of the burden. My aged father simply said, "If Mother agrees, so I also." At first Father Frank was concerned that my parents might hold my vocation against him, but gradually he and other Jesuits became welcome guests in our home, coming often for tea. Delicacies were first set before Buddha and then served to the guests in a pagan rite that might make the food prohibited for Christians. But the Jesuit guests, putting aside any case of conscience, scooped up the noodles with gusto.

The Provincial in California agreed to accept me at the Novitiate on the condition that I pay my own passage to California. Father Frank also had a solution for this financial problem. He made an appeal to the readers of *Jesuit Missions,* and generous benefactors sent me more than enough money. During this time, my seventy-seven-year-old father became ill. As he lay dying, I asked him, "Papa, wouldn't you want to enter the same heaven with us, so that we can be united again one day, all of us in one big, happy family?" Signs, rather than words, sufficed as tokens of a wish to be baptized; my father nodded assent. Father Frank was there to baptize him, giving him the appropriate name of Francis.

Shortly afterward, Father Frank visited the hospital and, approaching his bed, he asked in a whisper how my father was. Choking back tears, I embraced Father Frank, replying, "You are my father now." We prayed together, "May Francis Wong rest in peace." With the funds from my benefactors, I was able to pay for the funeral, sparing my brother at least this expense.

✣ 6 ✣

The Divine Romance
of Two Vocations

*I*N PREPARATION FOR *entering the Society of Jesus, twenty-year-old George Wong would take courses at Aurora University. Founded by the French Jesuits and funded in part by the French government, the university offered a curriculum leading to the French baccalaureate; all courses, with the exception of Chinese literature and foreign languages, were taught in French. Located halfway between the Jesuit compound Zikawei in the French concession and Shanghai, Aurora University was well known for its medical, dental, and law schools as well as for its library of sixty thousand volumes. There was very little reading material in English.*

Not long after George Wong had declared his intent to follow his mentor Father Francis Rouleau in religious life, he met and fell in love with Gladys Wei, the young woman assigned as his mother's catechist. Although they disclosed their vocation plans to one another and in doing so found themselves to be kindred spirits, the relationship was confusing. On the one hand, they were able to share a friendship that was about their mutual desire to serve the Lord and included an interest in the same books and magazines. On the other hand, Gladys not only felt that she could not accept George's invitation to join him at the movies; she found it necessary to write him a letter curtailing all contact between them. Prior to receiving Gladys's devastating letter, George confided to his spiritual father that he was preoccupied with Gladys, thinking of her too often, writing to her too often, and telephoning her too often; George's behavior was that of love's contemplative who just wanted to go on thinking of her.

Their relationship was salutary, providing him with the anima at the right time in his life's journey to get in touch with his feelings and make the yin connection with the earth and providing her with the animus that could open the sky to find impersonal truth revealed. The wounding effect of her letter enabled him to turn to his innermost feelings and acknowledge his vulnerability. For her it was a time to stand strong and erect. Father Rouleau did not encourage this breakup; rather, he wisely patched things up between George and Gladys. The result was their personal integration of the yin and the yang in the enduring friendship of companions for eternity.

✣   ✣   ✣

UPON THE DEATH of my father, my mother wished to receive instruction in the Catholic faith. A catechist was found in Gladys Wei, the spiritual daughter of Father Stanislaus Fitzgerald, also a California Jesuit. I had noticed Gladys at daily Mass but was not acquainted with her. She was seven years my senior. She came from a Protestant family but was educated by French nuns, the

Helpers of the Holy Souls, who operated within the bounds of the Sacred Heart parish and received the ministrations of the Jesuits.

Gladys spoke English, French, Cantonese, and Mandarin fluently and worked as a secretary in an office not far from my own. She was interested in my books and magazines, some of which had been sent to me from California by Father Frank's brother Ed, who corresponded with me regularly. She read my twelve issues of *The Sacred Heart Messenger* from cover to cover, but she turned down my invitation to go to the Cecil B. DeMille film *The Crusades*. We were kindred spirits, and I suspect that my mother, who didn't fully understand the idea and implications of a vocation, may have viewed us as potential marriage partners. Gladys and I, however, had disclosed to each other our vocation plans—she was preparing to join the Sisters of Social Service—so theoretically at least there was no misunderstanding between us about our intentions.

I began my studies at Aurora University, returning home by trolley a couple of times a week. The hardest part about Aurora University was that it was under the direction of the French Jesuits, whom I found rather strict; they lacked the easygoing style of their confrères from California. And perhaps the French Jesuits, who would have preferred that I do my novitiate with them, weren't pleased about my preparing to leave for California.

At any rate, the money from my benefactors covered the tuition for my Latin and Chinese studies at Aurora. Moving there, although I had spent my childhood in boarding school, was my first step at leaving home as an adult. For a while I had a room with a family, and then I moved into a university room with three other students. Father Frank came by bicycle to visit me my very first day at Aurora, and thereafter we saw each other frequently, at least twice and often three times a week. Knowing that I belonged to Christ, then and always, I was able to bare my soul's secrets to Father Frank, whose spiritual direction, marked with discernment and kindness, kept me encouraged.

On my visits home, I was always happy to see Gladys. She was a little short and rather thin, even bony, and she had a pleasant face and good teeth; what impressed me the most was her kindliness. Gladys came to our house to give religious instruction to my mother, not to talk to me, but we ended up talking. She was quite likable, and I visited her in her sister's home more than once.

On one occasion in my house, I took Gladys to my room to show her my library. When I told Father Frank about it, he explained, without any blame or admonition, that it wasn't customary for a young man to invite a young lady to his room. On another occasion, I frankly acknowledged to him, almost as a confession, that I thought about Gladys too much, that I wrote to her too often, and that I telephoned her too often. He did not suggest that I cut off relations with Gladys; in fact, he said, "You know, this is a very frank statement." He, in a lighter mood than I, told me I would know what I had to do and simply to live accordingly.

However, Gladys, after one of our visits, sent me a letter announcing, for our mutual benefit, the end of our friendship. I was devastated. To this day I do not know why she wrote me that letter; I am sure that I must have said something flippant that offended her. Maybe I complimented her, but, if so, it would have been about her, character, for I am certain that I wouldn't have made any reference to her looks. I tried to rationalize that Gladys was now showing a different face; this is a Chinese expression meaning that she might not have been so happy that day, that she had turned the face around.

I tried to tell myself that with Gladys there was no monkey business or halfway vocation. All I knew was that I would miss her very much, and really and truly I blamed myself for upsetting her, although I wasn't sure what I had said or done. The thing of it was that I was exceedingly tormented, unable to eat or sleep. There had been no discussion, just this letter abruptly curtailing the relationship. On the one hand, my reaction betrayed my weakness; on the other hand, it demonstrated that Gladys was not just a common friend. I wrote to

Gladys that I didn't understand her strict attitude, and I talked all this over with Father Frank. He spoke to Father Fitzgerald, her spiritual father, eventually patching up the friendship between Gladys and me.

A date was set for Gladys's departure for Los Angeles, where she would join the Sisters of Social Service. I went to the dock on the designated day to see her off, but she didn't show up. The next morning I saw her at Mass, her face and eyes all puffy and red. I blurted out, "What is the matter, Gladys? Have you got a cold?" What had happened was that her brother, to prevent her from leaving Shanghai to become a nun, had locked her in her room the day before; she had been up all night crying.

Gladys and I continued to see each other, and then one day she did not show up for Mass. It may have been Father Frank who told me, for her situation was an open secret in the Jesuit Community, or it may have been her sister. At any rate, in 1938 Gladys managed to leave for Los Angeles. I was not angry that she had not said good-bye, but perhaps I was a little hurt. My mother asked why I didn't just get married; I explained to her that I was planning to get married in California when I entered the Society of Jesus. There was the spiritual marriage of our vocations, Gladys's and mine, and there was the spiritual friendship we shared, a romantic friendship that would grow over the years, nourishing my vocation and providing a great source of inspiration and consolation in my imprisonment.

✢ 7 ✢

Love Jesus with All Your Heart

*B*Y THE TIME *George Wong left for his novitiate in 1939, the friendship he enjoyed with Father Rouleau was a brotherly bond based on love. In Confucian terms, the relationship was like that of the elder brother and the younger brother. The deathbed baptism of the senior Wong followed by the baptism of Mother Wong was more than an initiation into the church; it played a profound role in uniting two cultures and two families invited to share in the grace of the universal hurch. Father Rouleau was accepted into the Wong family, and the Rouleaus in California would extend the same familial welcome to the Jesuit novice from Shanghai.*

Father Rouleau had sent letter after letter to Provincial Francis Seeliger urging him to accept George Wong—openhearted, unsophisticated,

*joyous, innocent, intellectually brilliant, able to speak English, French,
and Chinese—as a novice. Both the Chinese language and the culture
were in his blood. Father Rouleau saw in him the kind of Jesuit his confrère
George Dunne had suggested for the China mission: a professional in
his particular field, in good health, fluent in Chinese, integrated into
the Chinese culture, and able to forego the comfortable aspects of
American life. He was well aware of the sacrifices made not just by the
novice himself, who had given up his job and left home, but by his whole
family. He also believed that his protégé would find that the Society of
Jesus would give more to him than he would give to the Society.*

*That same year, the Vatican issued the document approved by Pope
Pius XI—Father Rouleau would refer to it as the "Liberating Decree"
for China—that nullified the papal bull issued by Pope Benedict XIV in
1742, prohibiting the participation of native Chinese Christians in
Confucian and ancestral rites. The 1939 document also abolished the
oath of silence that missionaries had been required to take during the
previous two centuries regarding the Chinese Rites Controversy.*

❖   ❖   ❖

T HE CALIFORNIA PROVINCIAL, Father Francis Seeliger, had
indicated that I could begin my novitiate without delay. So
I gathered up just a few things to take with me to California—I
wouldn't need much—among which was a quilt that Gladys's sister
wanted me to mail to her once I arrived in the United States. On the
eve of my departure for California, my mother received baptism at
the hands of Father Frank. Then there was a farewell tea party at
which I, mindful of Jesus' words from the cross to the disciple John,
gave my mother to Father Frank and Father Frank to my mother. The
gist of the farewell message to my family was that rather than losing
a member, they were gaining a member. Father Frank took me to the
ship; he had arranged that Father Bob Dailey would come to our
house that evening to lift the burden of loneliness from my mother's

shoulders. How admirably Father Frank had realized the Chinese ideal of filial piety!

At the wharf, Father boarded the *Asama Maru*, a Japanese motor ship, accompanying me to my cabin. In a way suggesting the disciple before the beloved master, I knelt before Father Frank, who was sitting on my bunk. Feelings ran rather deep; the moment of leave-taking was too sacred for words. Then I broke the silence, blurting out, "Father Frank, love Jesus with all your heart!" I was embarrassed about this impulsive outburst. Who was I to be telling Father Frank to love Jesus? But Father Frank was a humble and wise master who overlooked this unwitting reversal of roles. He understood all that I had wanted to say.

Many years later, following my imprisonment, I described in a letter to Father Frank the humiliation I felt regarding my passionate appeal at our shipboard parting. I told him in this letter that I had always kept in my mind, and always would, the ideal he held up for me: to follow the gleaming goal of my vocation to the end, to be ever faithful in my love for Jesus and true in my love for him. I felt that our hearts had been knit as closely as those of Jonathan and David. In Father Frank, I saw mirrored, too, the apostle Paul's dedication to Christ. Certain that I could never match the length and breadth, the height and depth, of such surpassing love, I vowed still that as long as I lived I would love Love Incarnate in Father Frank and love Father Frank in Love Incarnate. I shall never forget Father Frank's reply to my letter, which after more than four decades of friendship, he read sitting in a wheelchair in Los Gatos. He said that, choked with emotion, he had cried like a baby.

During the twenty-three-day voyage across the Pacific, with stops in three Japanese ports and then in Honolulu, I looked forward to meeting Father Frank's elder brother, Ed, whom I referred to as Uncle Ed. The two brothers, both deeply religious, were very close and very supportive of each other, carrying on an intensely affectionate dialogue through frequent letters, some of them typed by me. Uncle

Ed had already come to know me fairly well; he wrote to me regularly during my days at Aurora University and kept me supplied with reading material. I also knew that the family referred to Father Frank not as Frank but as Francis, and it seemed to me that Francis was the more suitable name because of his gentlemanliness and warm disposition.

Sure enough, when I arrived in San Francisco, Uncle Ed was among those at the pier to greet me. With him were Father Pius Moore, the mission procurator in charge of the expenses of the missions of the California Jesuits in China, and Father Paul O'Brien, who is still living and doing good work in Thailand. It was September 2; Hitler had invaded Poland, and Churchill had declared war on Germany. Though at the time Americans had not entered the war, I was impressed by the patriotism of the newspaper boys stopping cars on the streets of San Francisco and hailing passersby as they shouted, "War is declared! War is declared!"

Uncle Ed took me sightseeing. We visited Golden Gate Park and the world's fair at Treasure Island. In the evening we took a Greyhound bus to Burlingame where I stayed with the Rouleau family: Uncle Ed and Aunt Mabel and their son and three daughters. Once, Uncle Ed confided that he was praying for a vocation among his son or daughters; it was Joan, the eldest, who, following the gleam, was to join the Sisters of Mercy in Burlingame to become Sister Mary Celeste. They were a wonderful, loving family, and the warmth and affection they offered me were truly appreciated and returned fervently. Just as Father Frank had come into my family in Shanghai, now I had come into his in Burlingame.

On Sunday, September 3, Uncle Ed took me to Mass at the University of San Francisco, where there was a special departure ceremony for three or four Jesuits going to China. I was introduced to Father William Dunne, president of the university, and had dinner there. Then Father Provincial Francis Seeliger drove me to the Novitiate in Los Gatos. It was dark when we arrived, and I asked him if I should present myself in his office the next day to register. He replied, "No, you begin tonight!"

And so, on September 3, 1939, I entered the Society of Jesus, asking Father Provincial if he had any advice for me. He answered simply, "Be generous." On Monday morning I awoke a bit homesick, not for China, but for Uncle Ed and his family in Burlingame, and yet I was happy to be at the Novitiate. I think I can fairly say that looking back, my years as a novice were the most pleasant of my life.

✢ 8 ✢

The Common Life

In 1939, GEORGE WONG entered the Society of Jesus, founded in Paris in 1534 by Ignatius of Loyola and his companions. It is an apostolic religious order of men whose vows of poverty, chastity, and obedience give them the freedom to pursue the fourth vow of serving in the vineyard of the Lord as missionaries wherever the pope chooses to send them. The expression and implementation of the fourth vow have seen variations both for historical reasons and because individual Jesuits have different politics, interests, and lifestyles. Nevertheless, there is the common theme of service to God through service to others and a common focus on the Good News that Jesus has come to set us free and make us more alive.

Jesuit life is about sharing. Jesuit priests share a common education that includes classical studies, philosophy, theology, and ministerial work. Probably having more bearing than education on shared language and shared experience is the Long Retreat that all Jesuits make at least twice. This thirty-day retreat consists of the Spiritual Exercises developed by St. Ignatius. Through meditation, contemplation, prayer, self-examination, and discernment, retreatants grow to experience God directly and in all things. The four weeks of the Long Retreat actually turn into a lifetime of continuous prayer, self-examination, decision making, and seeking God in the world.

Living with other Jesuits means more than sharing the experiences of everyday life; rather, it is a lifetime of shared experiences. When George Wong entered the Novitiate in 1939, he was beginning a personal relationship with Jesus Christ that would be a source of energy and confidence, that would develop like a calligraphic scroll into a continuous prayer, and that would be nurtured and challenged by his companions whether or not they were physically present.

Before the Japanese attack on Pearl Harbor on December 7, 1941, which marked the subsequent entry of the United States into World War II, novice George Wong received encouragement from Father Rouleau, whose letters were read aloud at Novitiate meals. When Father Rouleau was interned by the Japanese at Zikawei between 1942 and 1945, there were few letters. This was preparation for the spiritual communion that would begin in 1952 when Father Rouleau was expelled from China.

❖   ❖   ❖

ALTOGETHER I WOULD spend four years in Los Gatos, two years as a novice and two years in the juniorate; these would be followed by three years at Mount St. Michael's in Spokane, Washington, where I studied philosophy. At the Novitiate, we each had a cubicle for sleeping. After fifteen days there, we were given our cassocks. Everything was held in common, and we dressed alike with the same kind of jacket, the same kind of cap, the same work shoes for outside, and the same house shoes for inside.

Most novices had arrived in August on the eve of the Feast of the Assumption. We—there were twenty-five of us in the first year—picked grapes in the autumn and made our Long Retreat in November. We observed the seasons: Advent, Christmas, Lent, and Easter. Our daily program was regular and easy to follow. Rising at five, we went to the chapel for individual morning prayers. Each first-year novice had a second-year novice for an angel, someone to pray with him and show him the way. My angel actually left the order after seven years, joining the army. Brother Tom Hand was another companion; he is now spiritual director at Mercy Center in Burlingame.

One thing I had to work on when I arrived at the Novitiate was my English. Although I spoke the language fluently, I did so with a French accent, always emphasizing the final syllable. Moreover, I mixed up elements of standard phrases and sayings. For example, "raining cats and dogs" is an ordinary expression; I would say instead "raining dogs and cats."

We novices would kneel in the chapel and pray the way St. Ignatius taught us. It seemed easy enough to follow; my challenge was to apply the prayer to myself. We used the memory, then understanding, and then the will, making a personal application in relation to Our Lord. We considered how much we owed him, how we should love him, and how we should be loyal to him constantly, and generous as well. The meditation, from the Spiritual Exercises, on the life of Christ or on the particular feast day, would be divided into three parts. One of our brothers, the beadle who was a go-between for the brothers and the superiors, would ring a bell every twenty minutes or so to signal a change in posture. Kneeling, standing, sitting, we would pray for about an hour.

Our novitiate experience included picking grapes that would be made into sacramental wine. Each one of us had to cut grapes, as many as possible, and place them in a wooden box; a box represented a standard unit of sixty pounds. Some of the novices were really adept, able to collect one hundred boxes in one day. My first year, I brought in thirty boxes a day; my yield doubled the second year. The master of novices moved with us in the vineyard, admonishing us to speak in Latin, although we were able to speak to him in English as he seized the occasion to inquire individually about our spiritual life.

We took turns helping in the scullery. There was the table to be set, and there were dishes to be washed. Two brothers would fold the tablecloths, which were used at lunch and dinner but not at breakfast, which was served on the bare wooden table. During meals there was always some form of edifying reading from Scripture or from classic literature or perhaps from an article written by a Jesuit, one of Ours, as we referred to ourselves. Oftentimes passages of my letters from Father Frank were read aloud because of their strong spiritual character.

There was very little superfluous conversation at mealtimes. In Latin we might ask for the salt or for water, but there was no chatter except on special feast days, when Father Rector, then David Dazé, would proclaim, *"Deo gratias et Mariae,"* and we would answer, *"Semper Deo gratias,"* and then begin to talk with great animation. At birthday celebrations a box of chocolates was passed around. Feast days were truly festive with bright and beautiful flowers on the altar, their perfume mingling with the fragrance of the sacramental wine. Meals were carefully prepared and served, and we savored the luxury of ice cream on these occasions.

Feast-day evenings included lively dramatic and musical performances by our brothers. These little surprises—the flowers, the blossoming talent in the entertainment, a special song sung from the heart with gladness, the spontaneous laughter and applause, the meticulous attention to a holiday menu—all contributed to the bonding that came from living together and sharing joyful experiences with our brothers in Christ, something Father Frank had prepared me to do. It is quite a thrill to see Christ in others.

Once a week we had villa day. After breakfast and scullery, we changed our clothes and were assigned two companions. Then, in groups of three we walked down the hill, across the gully, over the creek, and up the hill to the Villa Joseph. It was a happy, informal time for conversation, but we tried to keep to spiritual or edifying topics. During the week, we joined our companions for conversation after meals, and then at the end of the week, we would tell one another any points we had observed in each other that could stand improvement.

To an outsider, these sessions might seem embarrassing or unduly humiliating, but in general they were helpful in making us aware of our need to be punctual or to speak charitably to others, for example. If arguments existed, we made an effort to look for the sincerity and good intentions of the speaker, coming to realize that the arguments were mostly based on personal opinion. The opportunity existed to consider opinions generously while distinguishing the opinion from a fact or from a form of absolute truth. So we may have argued with each other, but the point was to do so with kindness.

If something bothered us about someone and we didn't feel we could approach the individual, we were able to talk to Father Master Joseph King. I know that I felt hurt once when a companion called me a Chink, but he had not meant to be mean and, in fact, had always acted very kindly toward me. My spiritual task was to understand that his nickname for me was the result of a lack of consciousness and to find Christ hiding in him. That was not hard to do. Later on, much greater challenges would come in the search for Christ in prison guards and others, but these challenges or sufferings would also be a sacrifice, that is, a gift to Our Lord.

In the Novitiate on Saturday evenings, the beadle would announce in Latin, "*Fratres, tempus est,*" or "Brothers, it is time," meaning that the hour had come for corrections. Each second-year novice was subject to the criticism of the community of novices in an exercise we facetiously called the charity ball or *lapidatio*. *Lapidatio* refers to stone throwing as when Our Lord said, "Let the one among you who is without sin be the first to throw a stone" (John 8:7). The difference was that our virtual stones were thrown with love for our benefit.

So the one to be castigated or criticized would stand in the center of the room with the rest of us standing against the walls. Someone would begin: "It seems to me, Brother—I can only judge from appearances and don't know the motive—that you have been rather slow in your actions." Most learned to accept this kind of criticism that, as I have said, was offered in love for the improvement of the fellow Jesuit. It was also possible for one of us to ask to make a culpa, accusing ourselves of some infraction and then resolving in the presence of our fathers and brothers to make amends. Some people might compare these criticism or culpa sessions to the struggle sessions in Communist China, but there is a major difference. The Communist struggle sessions, devoid of love, are designed to beat people into conformity rather than to help them be the best they can be.

My two years of juniorate, when we had classes in English, Latin, Greek, and history, were somewhat more stressful for me than the two years of novitiate. I had a rather boisterous English teacher, Father John Brolan, who referred to me as a "screwball Chinaman," adding in the same breath, "I only kid the ones I like." For him, it was all a joke, so I tried to take it in a humorous vein.

Sacred oratory was also a part of the curriculum in the juniorate, and we gave sermons formally in the refectory. I gave my first one on the feast day of St. Francis Xavier, December 3. First I had to write it out and then correct it. I brought up how St. Francis Xavier was praying at the time of his death on the little island of Sanchian, south of Macao. He could see China but was not able to reach it and so was resigned to God's holy will. My teacher, extremely precise about the choice of words, objected to the word *resign* because of its passive nuance. Rather than resign himself to God's will, St. Francis Xavier would have embraced his disappointment; he would have actively given himself up to the will of God.

In our second year of juniorate, the oratory was to be in Latin. Mine was about the cure of the blind man in John's Gospel. I could tell that my Latin teacher was not impressed, but I did what I could. Less formally, we practiced oratory in class once a week. On one occasion, when I had both the formal preparation and the class preparation, I became tongue-tied in class. The teacher mercifully overlooked my poor performance that day.

As I found the regime as a junior somewhat demanding, I needed to rest after lunch. Also, as my eyesight seemed to be suffering, I was sent to an optometrist who prescribed glasses. However, one of my teachers gave me a book entitled *Sight without Glasses*. He suggested that I work on controlling my nervousness, and he seemed to be right. I got along without glasses until the age of forty-five when in the labor camp I requested a magnifying glass from home.

The next three years were spent doing philosophy in Spokane. At Mount St. Michael's, affiliated with Gonzaga University, I completed my bachelor's degree in English and my master's degree in philosophy. My master's thesis was on Lin Yutang, a contemporary philosopher in China whose books, including *My Country and My People*, became best-sellers in the United States in the 1940s. Although he was a good scholar and wrote some fine essays, I found his writing sometimes superficial and even hedonistic.

The greatest joy of my years in Spokane was joining Father Frank in a reunion with his brothers and their families in Yakima, Washington, on January 6, 1946. As a Jesuit novice, I had pronounced my first vows in 1941, and then came the Japanese attack on Pearl Harbor, blasting hopes for peace and resulting in conditions that made regular correspondence all but impossible. Father Frank was interned at Zikawei under the Japanese between 1942 and 1945. A few brief messages were delivered through Red Cross channels, but I missed the continuing support and encouragement that regular correspondence with Father Frank had brought me.

In Spokane at the end of my studies, I was thrilled to learn that the war was over and equally thrilled to learn that Father Frank was in the United States on furlough. Overjoyed to see him in Yakima, I found him thin and gaunt as a result of the hardships and low rations of the war, but beaming in the presence of his family. It was a great privilege to serve at the Solemn High Mass he celebrated on the Feast of the Epiphany, a prologue to the years of service and priestly sacrifice that lay ahead.

In 1946, Father Frank was assigned to Rome for further research in Chinese mission history, and I was to return to China. First I spent a few weeks in Los Gatos, and I also made a trip to Los Angeles to visit some of my benefactors as well as Father Frank's sister and her husband. Then, awaiting departure for China, I spent the rest of the summer with other Jesuit missionaries, taking a course at the University of San Francisco on the history of the Far East. St. Ignatius High School used to be located next to the university; we stayed there, putting mattresses on desks for sleeping. As a dockers' strike was going on along the Pacific coast, we did not have a firm date for departure.

Finally, word came that we could board a converted warship, the S.S. *Marine Lynxx*, on September 29, the Feast of St. Michael the Archangel. The six of us Jesuits—Father William Ryan, Brother James Finnegan, and four scholastics who included George Vincent Donahue, who would die in a tragic accident in Taiwan; John Clifford, who would be imprisoned in China; Frederick Foley, who would eventually leave the Society; and myself—found ourselves in the company of four hundred Protestant missionaries and four Catholic nuns. One of the nuns was Gladys Wei.

❖ 9 ❖

A Prophet in His Own Land

*I*N *1946,* THE *Jesuit scholastic returned to his homeland and was sent to the Maison Chabanel in Peking to master Chinese. The school took its name, ironically, from a seventeenth-century French Jesuit missionary to the Hurons in North America. Noël Chabanel never learned the Huron language, and he actually developed a loathing for these people, whose customs he could not understand. In 1649, he was tomahawked to death, and his body was thrown into the river.*

Opened in 1937, the Maison Chabanel represented the first opportunity for the California Jesuits to study Chinese in a systematic manner in a two-year program. The first year consisted of spoken Mandarin, and the second year included written Chinese. Previously, language learning was haphazard, existing only for a particular mission, and

Jesuits of different nationalities were isolated from each other. By 1939, other religious orders were represented at the Maison Chabanel. Jesuit novices and scholastics from Sienshien were moved there in 1946 to escape Communist reprisals (between 1945 and 1948 one hundred Catholic missionaries were murdered by Chinese Communists). The student dormitories were rather spartan, without running water or central heating. There was very little contact with ordinary Chinese, although prominent Catholic laypeople invited groups of Jesuit students to their homes so that they could learn the etiquette of Chinese dining.

It was only in 1948 that the California Jesuits received their own mission territory, which took the name of Yangchow. It consisted of the Yangchow area itself, Ricci High School and Sacred Heart Church in Nanking, and Christ the King Parish in Shanghai. George Wong was sent to Yangchow, a city one hundred miles inland from the China coast on the west bank of the Imperial Canal, twenty miles north of the Yangtze River. It was a great walled city with a long history. Marco Polo lived there for three years when he served as Kublai Khan's governor, and a tombstone dated 1342, from which Father Rouleau obtained the rubbing in 1951, bears Christian symbols, including a Madonna and Child, believed to be the first example of Marian art in China. Jesuits Matteo Ricci and Lazzaro Cattaneo passed through the city in 1598. Having established the mission in 1615, Venetian Jesuit Julio Ateni converted Mandarin Ma Sanqi and his son, to whom Ateni taught Euclid's geometry. Italian Jesuit Giovanni Domenico Gabiani arrived in Yangchow in 1660 and built the first church there. Nineteenth-century Jesuits established a clinic, and in the twentieth century, French and Chinese Jesuits, along with diocesan priests, cared for schools and dispensaries as well as the clinic.

However, Yangchow was not known for its conversions. The city itself had a population of three hundred thousand, mostly Buddhists, with only eight hundred practicing Catholics. Another two thousand

*Catholics in this city—which had resisted foreigners and Catholicism—
were considered rice Christians, that is, Christians more motivated by
the advantages of their religious affiliation than by genuine discipleship. When George Wong arrived in Yangchow to do his regency
(regency refers to the period a Jesuit scholastic "reigns" in the classroom
as a teacher), there were six residential mission stations, a high school
for boys and one for girls, nine primary schools, and a clinic. The mission had stocks in AT&T, Cenco, Firestone Tires, Gulf Oil, Continental,
Mapco, Tenneco, Textron, Union Pacific, and Winn-Dixie. The plans to
improve and expand services were curtailed with the advance of the
Communists.*

*Even Chiang Kai-shek acknowledged in 1948 that his own
Nationalist Party was decrepit and degenerate, lacking in spirit and
discipline and standards of right and wrong. Whereas he relied on the
loyalty of his cronies and fought an unpopular civil war against the
Communists, the Chinese Communist Party redistributed land and
equalized wealth and power in the rural regions and revitalized industry and commerce in the cities. The Communists were determined to
take over the buildings—orphanages, hospitals, churches, chapels, seminaries, and schools—operated by foreign missionaries in China; nearly
thirty-three thousand buildings were owned and operated by Catholics.
Jesuits had responsibility for one-sixth of the Chinese Catholic popula-
tion. Of the 888 Jesuits in China, 36 were from the California Province.
In 1948, Jesuit General Jean-Baptiste Janssens ordered all Jesuits
in China to remain there; he did not want the shepherds to abandon
the sheep.*

*The People's Liberation Army entered Shanghai on May 14, 1949,
taking possession of government buildings and police stations while
encouraging the people to go on with their lives. Bishop Ignatius Kung
Pin-mei ordained Jesuits in 1950 and again in 1951; George Wong was
in the last group to be ordained. Prime Minister Zhou Enlai announced*

that missionaries would be allowed to remain although no new missionaries would be admitted. Churches in China were to become fully indigenous. Church properties were being confiscated, and land was turned over to the peasants. In 1950, Christ the King Parish was taxed eighteen hundred American dollars in addition to other taxes. The following year saw the arrest and imprisonment of Monsignor Eugene Fahy, the apostolic prefect of the Yangchow district; the humiliating expulsion of the Vatican internuncio Antonio Riberi; and the brutal beating death of Jesuit Beda Tsang in Ward Road Prison.

Bishop Kung, openly defiant, organized a devotion to the Sacred Heart for young men in Shanghai. Police surrounded the cathedral as three thousand young men prayed inside and one thousand women recited the rosary in the square outside. The bishop had told his followers not to cooperate with the Communists and not to register as members of the Legion of Mary, a religious organization that the government declared a subversive society engaged in espionage. In spite of Communist action and reprisals that included arrests by the thousands with show trials and executions at the Shanghai racecourse, Catholics flocked to Christ the King Church, to St. Peter's Church (the former Aurora University), and to St. Ignatius at Zikawei.

The Chinese Catholics came forward to extend great care to the Jesuit missionaries, whose funds had been cut off and who were living on alms; groups like the Legion of Mary flourished. Charges in 1951 against the Jesuits included that their training, according to the methods of Ignatius Loyola, transformed them into machinelike tools of the church, that their Superior General was called the Black Pope, and that they took a special vow of obedience to the pope. Father Rouleau, continuing his research, teaching, and spiritual direction, underwent grueling interrogation sessions without his hearing aid (spare parts for it were not available). It is plausible that his hearing impairment persuaded the Communists that he could not possibly be a spy. Ready to face prison or *execution, he was summoned again one day in June 1952, issued an exit visa, and told to get out of China on the next train. Father Rouleau wrote to his brother, Edward, from Hong Kong, asking him to pray for Bernard, who was almost certain to become a martyr.*

❖   ❖   ❖

MEETING UP WITH Gladys was a total surprise. Unlike other Catholic nuns at that time, the Sisters of Social Service did not wear habits with the wimple covering most of the head and with skirts flowing to the floor. Rather progressive in their dress, they had something called a uniform. Their long hair was rolled into a bun, and for travel, they had hats with very short veils. They wore gray, midcalf-length skirts and gray blouses with collars and cuffs of white organdy. The gray Benedictine scapular, covering the crucifix, was cinctured by a thin black belt at the waist. Each sister wore the medal of the Holy Spirit—the dove and the flames. On deck they would don gray berets or go hatless; at Mass they wore black veils. Reminding me to call her by her religious name, Sister Candida, Gladys agreed to spend some time with me each day reviewing Chinese. After a couple of days at sea, however, her superior warned her that she was spending too much time with me, so our meetings ceased. That did not matter; we were both glad to be returning to our homeland to carry out our apostolates.

Although I had never been homesick for Shanghai during my seven years in the United States, I was now especially looking forward to seeing my mother. Reaching the coast of China after the fifteen-day voyage along the northern route, we could see the city of Shanghai from the deck, but the ship was not allowed to dock immediately. In fact, we waited several long hours. It was rather like being on a flight home after a long absence and having to circle the airport for a few hours rather than land. Finally, at eight in the evening, the boat docked and I was able to see my brother and one sister briefly; my mother had not come to the wharf. Gladys's family was there, greeting her and the sisters with great fanfare—it was her birthday, although the sisters didn't realize it because they celebrated feast days instead of birthdays—and whisking them all away in a limousine.

We Jesuit missionaries went off to Christ the King Church for dinner. Now overcome with homesickness, I wasn't interested in eating, but I didn't want to bother the superior, Father Paul O'Brien, with any special requests, and I didn't know my mother's telephone number. Much later in life, as we reminisced about those days in China, I told him how anxious I had felt that evening. Although it hadn't been my intention to be critical, Father O'Brien apologized about having been so insensitive; he simply had not taken into consideration that for one of the arriving missionaries, Shanghai was home. As I knew he was preoccupied, I kept quiet during dinner and went with the others to spend the night at the Jesuit house at Zikawei. Hearing that Hungarian Father Laszlo Ladany (who besides being an accomplished violinist was to become a well-known scholar regarding the church in China) needed an acolyte for Mass at the Carmelite convent the next day, I volunteered. When Mass was over, I took a pedicab to visit my family, staying with them for fifteen days. Very rarely in my life have I experienced such agitation as that first night back in Shanghai. I recall regarding it as a taste of purgatory or, at least, an opportunity to practice the virtue of patience.

In those days, Jesuit formation generally went like this: two years of novitiate, two years of classic studies and oratory during the juniorate, three years of philosophy, three years of teaching or regency, three years of theology followed by ordination, and then the fourth and final year of theology and tertianship (the period after ordination but prior to final vows). After the two-week visit with my family, I flew to Peking to do two years of Chinese studies at the Maison Chabanel directed by Père Georges Marin, a native of Massachusetts who belonged to the Province of the French Canadians. Father Marin's vision for the Maison Chabanel was that the school would not teach just the language but the culture of the Chinese people as well. We made excursions to places of interest like the Lama Temple, the Imperial Palace, the Temple of Heaven, the Winter Palace, and the Astronomical Observatory, which featured instruments used by Father Ferdinand Verbiest in the seventeenth century. But the cultural experience did not include much contact with local people and local customs.

In 1947, Chinese New Year fell on January 22 on the solar calendar. For weeks in advance, people prepared for the event by shopping, cleaning house, and settling debts, as it is a Chinese custom to settle debts on New Year's Eve. On New Year's Day all of the shops closed, and business was suspended for several days. In the temples, however, there was much coming and going as worshipers made supplications to the gods of prosperity. The folks in the streets were dressed in their best holiday clothes, mostly gaudy, and little children were dolled up like painted cherubs. Schools and colleges closed for three weeks' vacation, but we language students used this time to make our annual eight-day retreat with no extra holidays. It was a time of interior quiet for us, but outside there was noise galore—the *boom-bah, bi-blak-bi-blak* of firecrackers.

We were fortunate to have coal stoves in our rooms at Chabanel; not having heat during that cold winter would not have been conducive to study. So we learned and made progress, *jin-bu,* as we let ourselves be corrected endlessly and yet unashamedly. It was pleasant to live among very bright and cheerful Jesuit brothers at the Maison Chabanel, not all of them there for language studies. Some sixty Chinese novices and philosophers had fled their mission in Sienshien because the Communists were harassing them unmercifully. Religious persecution by the Communists was rampant despite the official pronouncement that there was religious freedom. Churches were being confiscated even in 1947, and missionaries were being put into prison on trumped-up pretexts.

During that period, a movie called *The Sacred City* was released. Combining fact with fiction, it portrayed the life of an American Catholic missionary, Father King, who worked for and with the Chinese people during the turmoil of the Sino-Japanese War and who was brutally murdered by the Japanese. The whole production was initiated by the Chinese. Technically, the film was below Hollywood's perfection; historically, it marked an era in the Chinese world plagued by atheistic Communism and promised the Catholic faith as an antidote. A box-office success, it was certainly a tribute to the Catholic missioner.

Interestingly, a few years before my stay at the Maison Chabanel, Père Pierre Teilhard de Chardin was in residence while he worked at the Chinese geological survey. Apparently he didn't get along with Père Marin, though he was well liked by everyone else. Père Teilhard never really bothered to learn Chinese, but unlike Marin, he is said to have grown close to the Chinese soul. When I began my language studies, Father Frank was delighted that, unlike the other missionaries from abroad, including himself, I would have both a facility with the language and a native sense of the culture. Because of the language studies, my regency was shortened by two years and was to be spent in Yangchow. In fact, in the autumn of 1948, when my one-year regency had just begun, the advance of the Communist armies caused our superior, Father Eugene Fahy, to send my companions from California back to Alma College in Los Gatos for their theology studies (eventually they would go to Taiwan as missionaries, as did Father Fahy) and me to Shanghai for mine.

We had been in Yangchow for only three months, barely enough time to learn the names of our pupils. And yet many things had happened, including the unexpected death of one of the Jesuits, William O'Leary, whom we called Jeeps. There was a lot of personal feeling surrounding his death as we had picked grapes together, walked to the Villa Joseph together on villa days, said the rosary together, and had our recreation together under the novices' tree in Los Gatos. A quiet fellow, he had grown especially communicative in Yangchow as he was excited about school preparations. I had come to know and like him better.

The day before he died, Jeeps was terribly sickly looking and had been taken to the Protestant hospital. They were quite friendly to us, but there was no bed for Jeeps. The doctor said that his ailment was nothing serious; he recommended light foods, vitamin pills, and quinine. Back at our house, a bed was fixed for him in the library. He lay there with pains in his sides. Hot-water bags were applied to ease his suffering, and as his condition deteriorated, he was given some brandy to ease his breathing. For a little while the brandy seemed to help, but then his breathing became more labored. Artificial respiration was administered. Father Bill Ryan, appearing on the scene, said that Jeeps was dying; he told Father Philip Oliger, known because of his age as Pop, to give him absolution. Pop did so, yelling at Bill to give Jeeps extreme unction as he went to call the doctor, this time from Providence Hospital. Bill took the oils and began anointing Jeeps's forehead as he shouted into his ears, "I'm giving you extreme unction! Are you sorry for your sins?" Jeeps's eyes flickered, and he breathed his last. Sacerdotally clothed, he was buried in a Chinese coffin behind the church. The doctor, a Chinese who was Western trained, said that it was an acute case of cerebral meningitis. It came on so suddenly and unexpectedly; Jeeps was only thirty-four years old when Our Lord called him home.

In Yangchow, I lived also with Father Francis Xavier Farmer, whom I had first met when I was only seven years old when he officiated at the funeral of my sixteen-year-old cousin. A man of exemplary faith, Father Farmer had been interned by the Japanese along with Father Frank at Zikawei between 1942 and 1945. In Yangchow, he enlivened our meals more than the food did, and when the food was topped with Los Gatos wine, he would wax eloquent about the past. Once he described how he had refused communion to a scantily clothed young girl—in those days, signs were often posted in the entryway of a church as reminders that even in hot weather sleeveless dress was inappropriate—telling her to return properly attired to attend the Lord's banquet. She complained to him, or in the words of Father Farmer, she appeared for redress. I think that she actually did go home, change her clothes, and come back.

On another occasion, I informally sought some personal information from him for a write-up for *Jesuit Missions*. About seventy years old, Father Farmer was a convert from Georgia who had once been a Methodist missionary in China. His wife, also a Methodist missionary, had died a few years after the death of their infant son. Having returned to Georgia, he became a Catholic and entered the Society of Jesus in 1916 at the age of thirty-nine. A member of the Province of Paris, he had his novitiate in England. After his ordination, Father Farmer spent a year at the Maison La Colombière in Paray-le-Monial, France, in preparation for being sent to China. Opening up like a flower in bloom (his Chinese name suitably was *Hua*, which means flower), he shared with me some details about his home leave to the States in 1946.

Père Yves Henry had favored Father Farmer's going to visit his mother but had no power to authorize the trip. Moreover, Père Georges Marin told him that it was not edifying for a Jesuit to ask such permission; this statement amounted to *no*, which Father Farmer accepted with humility. But word had reached his mother about our California men being able to go home for a rest; it was hard for her to bear not seeing him. Eventually, at the request of others, namely Fathers Joseph Verdier, Yves Henry, and Eugène Beaucé, Father Provincial Bith ordered him home to Atlanta. Not only that, the New Orleans Provincial—Father Farmer was under his jurisdiction during his stay in Atlanta—gave him permission to live with his mother as long as he was there. It turned out that he spent six blessed months with her, whereas in 1923, under orders from Paris, he had been allowed only an eight-day visit with his relatives in Georgia.

Of course, I did not include this anecdote in my article for *Jesuit Missions,* but I did hope to convey something of Father Farmer's exemplary spirit. He was always kind in his criticism; he never called anyone a piker or a fool, although, separating the actor from the act, he referred sometimes to mistakes as foolish. Eager to follow God's will in patience, hope, and delicate silence, Father Farmer was one of the happiest men I knew. Praising the young Jesuits who had arrived recently in China, he made it clear that he was happy to see me as a Jesuit also.

During those three months of regency, I continued my regular correspondence with Father Frank, who offered great support as I questioned my teaching ability and disciplinary leadership and complained about the Yangchow dialect and local conditions, such as the lack of flush toilets. While very encouraging, he suggested that I think less about my carcass and reminded me of the grace provided by Ignatian indifference. I resolved to be more like St. Paul, who rejoiced in his infirmities. And I offered Father Frank, whom I loved dearly, a suggestion to help him conserve his strength while preaching at three Sunday Masses, one after the other. I wrote to him that he should try to speak less loudly in church.

With my regency curtailed, I proceeded to Zikawei to begin theology in 1948. Even though 1949 saw the establishment of the Communist dictatorship in China, classes at the Jesuit seminary at Zikawei continued pretty much as usual for the next year. Father Frank, who had been on sabbatical in Rome, returned to Shanghai to become our professor of church history and China mission history. After three years of theology, I was nearing the climax of my vocation.

On May 31, 1951, as the first Chinese among the California Jesuits, I was ordained a priest by the first Chinese bishop of Shanghai, Ignatius Kung. I celebrated my first Mass at Sacred Heart Church in the parish of my boyhood with Father Frank assisting me at the altar. In the front pew, my mother knelt beside my brother and sisters, who, undaunted by the ominous political situation, kept their minds and hearts focused on the sacrament. More and more priests were being arrested and expelled, and church properties were being heavily taxed or simply confiscated. During the months before and after my ordination, the Vatican Internuncio, Antonio Riberi, was the target of a series of negative newspaper articles describing him as a running dog of the imperialists. The Communists would not simply expel him as a diplomat, charging him with obstructing government policy. On September 5, 1951, they searched his person, handcuffed him, and took him under guard to the train station, where he was put aboard a train bound for Hong Kong.

Persevering after ordination, I did my fourth year of theology studies and my tertianship. The tertian master was a French Jesuit, Père Coathalem, who spoke Latin to us and was rather strict about certain things. For example, I once attended a celebration on the Feast of Christ the King at the California Jesuit church dedicated to Christ the King with one of my classmates from California, Father John Clifford. Invited by the Californian pastor, Father Tom Phillips, to stay and celebrate the benediction, I made a telephone call to the tertian master. When I did not reach him, I left a message with another father about the benediction, presuming permission from the superior, Father Charles McCarthy. When I returned, I found a note from the tertian master castigating me for not notifying the superior about staying on for further service. This was a misunderstanding about presumed permission; the superior had not agreed explicitly to the benediction devotion. The French fathers were particular about these and other things.

My theology thesis, supervised by Père Coathalem, was a rebuttal to Leonard Feeney's interpretation of *extra ecclesiam nulla salus*, that is, that there is no salvation outside the church. Feeney, a Boston Jesuit, was a talented poet and, for a time, was literary editor of *America* magazine. As chaplain to Catholic students at Harvard and Radcliffe, he held the view that only an explicit profession of faith and entry into the Roman Catholic Church would secure salvation. This narrow view, contrary to church teachings, resulted in his being recalled by the Society of Jesus from his collegiate mission, but since he refused to respond to the recall, he was expelled from the Society of Jesus. Eventually he was excommunicated after refusing to appear in Rome when summoned there. (Happily, later in life Feeney was reconciled with the church.) In my thesis, I argued that Feeney neglected to appreciate the baptism of desire that could be considered an implicit profession of faith acceptable to a merciful God. The thesis had to be in Latin, and I was especially grateful to Father Charles McCarthy, who had become rector of the theologate, for help in this effort. The grade on the thesis was eight out of ten, but the score on my oral examination, also in Latin, was not sufficient for me to receive the licentiate of sacred theology. These results meant that my final vows would be simple rather than solemn, although even this changed at a later time when Vatican II brought a greater leniency into the Society, and my solemn vows were received.

Following my tertianship, I spent two years, from 1953 to 1955, concurrently teaching English at Zikawei Diocesan Seminary and serving as assistant pastor at Christ the King Church, which was located next to the Jinjiang Hotel, where President Richard Nixon would stay during his historic visit to China in 1972 (the church has since been demolished to give way to a new forty-four-story annex to the hotel).

It was in 1953 that my mother died at the age of seventy-four. As part of a Lenten mission, I had six days of sermons to prepare, but the mission was interrupted by her death on March 3, just at the beginning of a novena to St. Francis Xavier. Stalin died at the same time, so people were wearing black armbands; for me, those bands represented mourning for my mother although they were intended for Stalin.

Well acquainted with the gospel teaching about a prophet not being welcome in his own country, I had some trepidation about being a missionary in my homeland and preaching to my compatriots, but actually there was no reason to be nervous. People flocked to our parish, and fortunately, my experience of being tongue-tied in oratory class did not repeat itself in the pulpit. However, the tongues of some of the parishioners weren't silent either.

Sister Candida, Gladys Wei before her entry into religious life, was living in a convent adjacent to Christ the King Church. While still at the theologate, I would come to Christ the King two or three times a week to hear confessions between six and eight; after Mass, I joined Sister Candida for breakfast. On first Fridays I conducted devotions in the convent chapel. In fact, I found it convenient to meet with parishioners at the convent because a room was always made available for spiritual consultation, whereas we did not have enough room at the church and the rectory was always under police surveillance. Some of the people got wind of the fact that I had known Sister Candida before, and there was some concern about our relationship, about my having fallen head over heels for her. My superior, Father Vincent Chu, was not concerned, however; he simply asked me to keep him advised of when I was at the convent, and that was easy enough to do.

Under the Communists, priests were put under house arrest. Even so, I moved about quite freely, leaving my residence at the theologate or the tertian house or the rectory as the case might be. By 1953, all the American Jesuits had been imprisoned or expelled. While on sabbatical in Rome during the 1940s, Father Frank had collected lots of material, including films, photographs, and documents pertaining to mission history in China; then in Shanghai he acquired a microfilm viewer left behind by the American military. When it became apparent that he would not be able to conduct his work in China, Father Frank applied to go to the Philippines, where he would continue his research on the Chinese rites while teaching church history. But first he thought it best to burn some of the films; the originals in Rome could be duplicated again. One of the servants at the theologate reported to the Communist authorities that Father Frank had a big machine, so there was an investigation, but when the authorities realized it was just a microfilm viewer and not some instrument of espionage, they finally expelled him.

As foreigners were being imprisoned or expelled, native clergy were also being investigated. My first encounter with the interrogation process happened at Zikawei after a servant in the house who was not pleased with my manner contacted the police, who encouraged this kind of spying and reporting. I was kept up all night. At eight in the morning, a policeman took the interrogators aside and whispered something. I was ordered to my room on the third floor, then later ordered to move my room to the ground level. This may have been because one of our priests, Father Anthony Wang, had jumped from his window on the third floor to his death on the concrete below. Educated in Rome, he was our canon-law teacher and our first native Chinese theologian; the other professors were Austrian, French, German, Italian, and so on. Father Wang had told me of his concern about saying something incriminating. I had suggested that he say a prayer for strength and courage; I think his leaping to his death was an act of courage. He preferred to die rather than unconsciously cooperate with the Communists. He was given a full Christian burial, attended by the bishop.

In 1955, the doctor ordered the removal of my tonsils; the surgery was to be performed in the infirmary at Zikawei, which had an operating room that had not been used before. After being given an injection, I was to remain conscious during the tonsillectomy, which, as my screams would testify, was painful. But actually I had another reason to cry out: the operating table, unfortunately not assembled correctly, collapsed with me on it. Everybody in the infirmary heard my terrified cries. For the next three days my friends and caregivers pampered me and treated me to ice cream and cold drinks as I recovered in the room at Zikawei usually assigned to the visiting bishop.

Though I did not realize it then, I have come to understand that the tonsillectomy was a blessing; otherwise I might have suffered from infections during my years in prison and in the labor camp.

With Father Vincent Chu, the pastor, I continued in parish ministry at Christ the King Church. I heard confessions in the morning between six and eight, usually in English, as many of the Chinese Catholics of Shanghai had been educated by missionaries and felt more comfortable with English as their religious language. I then celebrated Mass, which was in Latin in those days, and we held the Benediction every evening. Father Chu and I realized that among the reasons for the good Mass attendance and active participation of the people in church life was that they had nothing else to do; the Communists had eliminated most distractions. Our religious-education program was thriving, with the teenagers giving catechism to the little children and with a series of sermons on church government and loyalty to the pope being offered in the evenings for adults.

Meanwhile, the Communists, while having done some good things like providing a stable currency (inflation had been rampant under the Kuomintang), closing down brothels, offering respectable jobs to reformed prostitutes, and putting some order in traffic, were conducting a vicious anti-Catholic campaign. In order to wipe out religion, the Communists believed that it was necessary to turn public opinion against charitable institutions. One tactic was the public condemnation of the Legion of Mary, a Catholic organization of laypeople united by prayer and good works. These devout people visited the sick and tended dying beggars, conducted catechism classes, and shared in devotions. The Communists officially considered the Legion of Mary a subversive society. Rounding up members, the authorities would incite them to cut off their association with the Legion, an action symbolized by stepping on a crucifix. Then they would insist on getting a report on other members. Men and women, teenagers and adults, went to prison for remaining loyal members of the Legion of Mary. In waging war against the Legion of

Mary, the Communists turned the very name of the organization, Legion of Mary, into a term of opprobrium; I even heard rickshaw pullers use the term as they cussed each other with grins on their faces.

The campaign to inflame public opinion against the Catholic Church was especially evident in its attack on the nuns who operated orphanages; they were accused of murdering babies through neglect. It was true that many of the babies brought to the orphanages died, but not because of the neglect of the sisters; these infants were sometimes already dead before they arrived at the orphanages. Recall that in 1937, Father Frank had observed that the Zikawei girls' orphanage received an average of 160 abandoned babies a week, most of whom died shortly after being picked up. He referred to them as the little Chinese baby saints in heaven. "The church in China is predominantly a baby church," he explained to his brother Ed in a letter I typed for him during the early days of our friendship. After the Communists took over, nuns were arrested, paraded through the streets in humiliation, and imprisoned.

The convent occupied by Sister Candida was a two-story house that had once belonged to a Portuguese family. A lot of publicity was accorded a police search that turned up some revolvers buried in the garden. With no consideration given to the possibility that the guns had been buried by the former occupants of the house, the implication was that the nuns were stocking and hiding weapons. Similar discoveries and accusations, implicit and explicit, were frequent in China.

In 1955, on September 8, the Nativity of Our Lady, Bishop Ignatius Kung of Shanghai was arrested, along with Father Vincent Chu, the pastor at Christ the King. The newspaper published as one of Bishop Kung's crimes that he said Mass "in honor of counterrevolutionaries." At dinner the evening before his arrest, Father Chu and I had talked about how active the parish was and about the contagious fervor of the Catholics. Then in the night—the police always came at night—he was arrested. Before being taken away, he knelt down before me, and said, "George, give me your blessing." The policemen drew their guns, asking why he was resisting. He replied that he was not resisting but simply asking for a blessing. Two weeks later it would be my turn.

George Bernard Wong as a Jesuit novice in Los Gatos, 1939.

Jesuits Wong, Donahue, Ryan, Foley, and Clifford at the Maison Chabanel in Peking, 1947.

Sister Candida (Gladys) Wei, date unknown.

Scholastic George Wong with Father Francis Rouleau, about 1949.

Father Rouleau at Mother Wong's birthday party, in George's absence, 1940.

✣ 10 ✣

Before Magistrates and Judges

*I*N 1953, WHILE *Father Wong was under house arrest, two of his companions from California were arrested and imprisoned. John Clifford actively fought the brainwashing methods of the Communists. Moral conviction characterized by an obligation to others was his motivation for resisting the efforts of his captors to get him to sign a false confession. He practiced the deliberate and constant strengthening of every human attribute the treatment of his captors sought to weaken. He recalled sunny and tender episodes of his life and retained a sense of humor even though there was little to laugh about. He abandoned his American gregariousness in order to cut himself off from group influence. Putting aside his Jesuit training to look for the best in others while calling to mind the Ignatian imagery that pits the standard of Lucifer against the* *standard of Christ, he consciously regarded his cell mates and the authorities as enemies.*

Thrown into momentary panic in isolation, Clifford made a habit of meditating on all the pleasant events of his life, all the joys and laughter, and most of all, the moments when his will triumphed over weakness. In time, he could sense the dawn and the smell of a rose and hear the laughter of his mother. Clifford "reread" all his favorite books, struggled with canon law, and reviewed the principles of dialectical materialism, which he found no more valid in prison than he had during his college days. When there was no sunlight, he was able to bring back the golden sparkle of the sea near San Francisco; where there was no darkness with the lightbulb burning night and day, he could feel the soft blackness of a night in the woods; and where there was only bestiality and meanness, he could recall the intellectual challenge of the University of Santa Clara, where he had once taught philosophy. He stretched out his prayers and meditations so that they lasted all morning, and he argued openly and boldly with his captors, insisting that they were the guilty ones for persecuting him because of his religion.

The obligation he felt to be an example to his Chinese students appeared as a leitmotiv of Clifford's experience. Before his arrest, he had promised them that he would not write a statement of any sort or sign his name to a confession. Besides being concerned that an unguarded admission might give authorities clues leading to their arrest and persecution, he did not want to fail those he had taught to resist what he considered to be the Communist violation of humankind. And though thinking about defiance caused his knees to tremble, he had before him the example of Father Beda Tsang, the wise and gentle Chinese Jesuit who went to jail with his usual jauntiness and confidence and was then tortured to death. So faith, conviction about doing what was right as an example to others, and alert stubbornness sustained Clifford. He argued with authorities, as when the guard, observing him through a peephole one morning, noted that his lips were moving. The guard admonished him for breaking the rules by praying. Clifford shouted back that it was the guard who had no right to arrest him, that the guard had no rights over him, and that he would go on praying.

California Jesuit Tom Phillips, imprisoned at the same time, was equally steadfast in his refusal to yield to the Communists, although his style was not confrontational. His Jesuit education, having exposed him to profound and complex ideas, helped him to recognize problems and gave him the mental resources to sit apart quietly and think or pray about something when necessary. Phillips had been in the process of carrying out a plan to create leadership in Christian education among young men and women in Shanghai following the rise of Communism; the ability of an instructed laity to function without priests would be important since the Communist method was to separate the priests from the laity.

One aspect of the plan included training Catholic students to be, as far as laypeople could, the priests' successors. These students received an intensive course on the significance and richness of their faith, the problems posed by the Communists, and the difficulties encountered in attempting to lead a Christian life. The first part of Phillips's plan included the delivery of a series of well-executed sermons on persecution and not rendering to Caesar what belongs to God. There was an emphasis on the Chinese character of the church in Shanghai; Chinese Jesuits organized, planned, and executed the whole course of sermons at Christ the King. People flocked to hear the sermons, and then they put their faith into action. A young doctor was arrested for refusing to accuse the sisters at the hospital of crimes against humanity, and his wife had to sell eggs in the street to survive. Parishioners bought up all her eggs for months ahead at higher than market prices, and they made sure that she and her children had food and medicine. This was not an isolated incident.

Like Clifford, Phillips found himself in prison thinking of the example he had to set for others. It was more difficult for him to think of his captors as enemies, but he did so with the understanding that the man interrogating him could maliciously contrive something he said in honesty and innocence into a lie that could mean his life or liberty, or the life or liberty of someone else. Still, he ardently taught a fellow prisoner, whom he was preparing for a clandestine baptism, that as a Christian he had to root all rancor and bitterness out of his heart and love the judge who sentenced him and the jailer who mistreated him.

Consolation came to Phillips in various forms: in the eagerness and docility of this convert to the grace of God; in a fellow prisoner bearing a chaplet fashioned from a knotted rag who, under the very eyes of the guards, was making it known that he was Catholic and praying for them all; in the rays of sunlight entering the cell; in hearing, in the early hours of Christmas, someone, somewhere outside the prison, playing "Puer Natus" on a Chinese flute; and through prayer. Consolation also came to both Clifford and Phillips, as to countless other priests, in the Eucharist, sometimes celebrated in what Father Wong would call the dry Mass, that is, without bread and wine, and sometimes with elements smuggled into prison.

Clifford and Phillips were released together in 1956. Clifford had not signed one paper; he even refused to sign his release documents and literally had to be thrown out of jail. In 1957, California Jesuits John A. Houle and Charles J. McCarthy were released from prison. Reports of Father Charles McCarthy following his release from the Chinese prison describe him as tense and nervous, and yet he claimed that, as bad as his treatment was, the treatment of the Chinese priests was far worse.

✢   ✢   ✢

ON SEPTEMBER 9, 1955, priests not in custody were rounded up and transported by car or taxi to a meeting hall where it was proclaimed that the ringleaders of the Catholic Church had been arrested the night before. We were lectured about the liberation and the new China, about Chiang Kai-shek and the pope, about American imperialism and the glory of Communism. Then we were instructed to discuss these things among ourselves. These sessions continued for the next two weeks at the local station where we would report after Mass and breakfast. Lunch was provided at the first meeting; afterward they had our cook send lunch. Even at the church I was cut off from contact with outside people, and I was questioned about finances and property.

Foreign monetary transactions were conducted privately, since transfers of funds were illegal. For example, many of the Shanghai people moving to Hong Kong left money at the church as they were not allowed to take money abroad. We would then give them a letter to be delivered to Italian Father Franco Belfiori, the Jesuit procurator in Hong Kong. The letter would acknowledge the receipt of a certain sum and request that an equivalent amount be granted to the bearer in Hong Kong dollars. This kind of private exchange was illegal even though no money had left the country. It enabled the parish to continue operating in spite of the outrageously high taxes designed to force the religious to abandon their buildings and their mission. I had been given a gold bar by the former superior, Father Paul O'Brien, worth about two thousand dollars. Not having any place to hide it, I confided it to a loyal Catholic family. Eventually, I revealed its whereabouts to the Communists who, of course, confiscated it.

The Communists were also confiscating church properties. The Passionists had photostatic deeds to their properties, Kuomintang documents, that they had entrusted to the Maryknoll fathers, who in turn gave photocopies to me. The danger was that possession of the deeds indicated a hope that the properties would one day be restored; this kind of hope was criminal as far as the Communists were concerned. I gave these papers to my brother, Willie, for safe-keeping. The police had been keeping watch on church residences, and they had actually used a telephoto lens to photograph the Maryknoll father when he came to visit me, bringing the photostatic copies with him. After questioning the Maryknoll father, who apparently admitted delivering the photostatic copies to me, the police came to interrogate me. When confronted with evidence that the photostatic copies were in my possession, I claimed that I had burned them. Later, I asked the superior what I should do. He said to go ahead and burn them, since that is what I had claimed. So I got the papers from Willie, and with the help of a Hungarian Jesuit brother, Gyorgy Csaszar, I burned the papers in a stove in our house one night in April, praying that the smoke rising from the chimney would not raise suspicions.

During those September interrogations at the police station, one of the cadres asked me about a job at the church. Before I could answer him, he insisted on knowing why we kept so much money and immediately launched into an attack of the bishop. "Your bishop is reactionary. He is anti-Communist, proimperialist. Just say that your bishop is an imperialist running dog." When I refused to sign any papers denouncing the bishop, I was told, "Go home!" When I got home, I made up a little bundle of things, for it was clear to me that I would be going to prison.

They came for me at eleven o'clock the night of September 26, 1955. "Get up!" they ordered. A rented car took me to Railway Station Jail, where political prisoners were held in custody. Wardens searched my person and inspected the partial dentures I had even then. They took my watch, my rosary, and my scapular medal. I had to sign an acknowledgment of my arrest, and then before midnight, I was assigned to a small cell on the third floor. Even though there was only one wooden plank on the floor, I shared the cell with another prisoner, a telegraph operator, who was perhaps in his late twenties or early thirties. We were not supposed to talk. As I wondered how we would sleep on the single wooden plank, I realized that I had forgotten to bring the bundle I had prepared.

There was a knock on the door, and I heard my name: One Three Two Seven. For the next seven years, between 1955 and 1962, I would be addressed as One Three Two Seven. I was summoned to a small room where a large sign proclaimed, "Leniency to those who confess; severity to those who hide." When I saw the four interrogators, I was reminded of my philosophy and theology exams; there were always four examiners, and they couldn't all ask questions at the same time.

The interrogation continued from half past midnight until half past one the next afternoon. At about six in the morning, I had a hard time not dozing off. They wanted to know all about my life, all my acquaintances, all my connections. They repeated, "Don't be afraid to confess. The more you confess the better. Don't try to hide anything." A written deposition covering my life, my work, and my relations was required.

Even though I knew that death was always a possible outcome and remembered vividly the example of the first Chinese Jesuit to die in prison at the hands of the Communists, Father Beda Tsang, I was not afraid; rather I was bolstered by his example. Moreover, I remembered Jesus' telling his disciples not to worry about being called before judges and magistrates as the Holy Spirit would furnish the words. I might have interpreted this passage as saying that, thanks to the Holy Spirit, eloquent speech would flow from the mouth, but that is not exactly the way it worked. I took comfort in John Henry Newman's saying not to worry about what you say as working against you because, in one way or another, it will eventually work in the Lord's favor. St. Paul also said that all things work together for good for those who love the Lord, so I did not agonize over my situation. Without searching for answers or probing for understanding, I simply knew, and deeply so, that I trusted God.

After that first interrogation in prison, I was allowed to return to my cell and even to sleep. A routine began of two meals a day: dry rice with some cabbage at eight in the morning and wet rice at four in the afternoon. There was a piece of pork, which is the staple in

China (Buddhist bonzes and Muslims were served an egg instead), a couple of times a week, although once, during a famine, we had fish rather than pork. Interrogations followed these meals, and they usually went on for two to three hours at a stretch as my written depositions were reviewed.

Mostly the questioning didn't bother me; the hardest thing to go through was talking about Father Frank. It was disgusting to speak of something so personal; he was innocent, a man devoted to service for others, but the Communists were more interested in his microfilm viewer. Talking to them about this dear friend was like feeding pearls to swine. However, I endured it, just relating facts that hopefully weren't compromising to anybody. The problem was that the Communists tried to mislead the prisoners, manipulating whatever they said, hoping to trip them up and to use whatever they said against themselves and others. Remembering John Henry Newman's insight, however, I got through the questioning about Father Frank.

Then they started in on my relationship with my sister-in-law, Julie; my brother, Willie, had already been demoted at his workplace because of his relationship to me. The questions were insulting to Julie's character and mine, implying that we were engaged in illicit relations. They asked about our being together alone and things like that. Once, during such a line of questioning, I grew angry and pounded my fist on the chair, exclaiming, "Why do you ask me these questions?" I was reprimanded for my disrespectful attitude toward the government's official and was sent off to write another deposition.

Up until then, I had been allowed to write my depositions in English, and quite intentionally I wrote long, complex sentences that would be difficult to translate. In all honesty, I don't think that the authorities held it against me that I was more comfortable with a foreign tongue than with my native language. After my outburst, however, I was told that since I was Chinese, I should write in Chinese. "Very well," I said, telling them that I would need a dictionary. I was

instructed to write to my church for a dictionary, and almost immediately, my dictionary from Zikawei appeared. It was a fine Chinese-
English dictionary compiled by a Protestant named Matthews. To
tell the truth, writing in my native language was a worthwhile exercise for me, although I am sure that my imperfect Chinese provided
the readers with some degree of amusement.

✣ 11 ✣

Priest and Victim

ONE EXAMPLE OF *a Chinese priest and victim is that of Jesuit Dominic Tang, appointed bishop of Canton in 1951, as the foreign missionaries were being imprisoned and expelled. The twenty-two years he spent in prison following his arrest in 1958 were marked by severe brutality. Quite typically he was deprived of sleep as he went through long hours of interrogation night after night. For long periods of time, he would be confined to a dark and dreary cell where he feared going blind. He suffered from the cold because his clothes were inadequate and threadbare. Questioned during his final prison days about being barefoot as he pulled weeds outside, Bishop Tang was not at liberty to explain that his only pair of shoes had worn out years before. He nearly starved to death in prison and was sometimes beaten by cell mates. On one occasion, deprived of his full meal by a hooligan cell mate who seized the meager strip of pork that was the only meat he had been given in years, he dared not report this treatment to the guards.*

There was no contact with the outside world, so he had no idea if his mother was living or dead. She died during his imprisonment; during the entire twenty-two years, he did not receive one letter from his relatives. With a couple of exceptions, he was not allowed to write to his family to request necessities like soap, clothing, or vitamins. One day, however, after an interrogation session, the judge told him that he could write to his mother in Hong Kong. Careful to write only a few simple lines, Bishop Tang sent his family his good wishes and gave his address as Wong Wah Road Prison. In order to put his mother's mind at peace, he said that he was studying in prison, although that was not true. Month after month and year after year, he waited for a response, but his letter was like a stone thrown to the bottom of the great sea.

During the Resist America–Help Korea campaign (1950–1952), three young girls whom Bishop Tang did not know came to interview him at his residence. He was living in a Carmelite convent as heavy taxation made it impossible to maintain the customary houses. The girls asked him if he thought the Korean War was a just war. He answered that he did not know if it was a just war and told them to work hard in their studies. He was accused by the authorities of holding the students back by not encouraging them to join the army. On a different occasion Bishop Tang agreed with another priest that since the business of capitalists was legal and they paid taxes, the confiscation of their property and the struggle against them were unfair. He was accused of opposing Communist campaigns spread over Canton, campaigns that began the systematic elimination of the middle class.

In 1957, the government started a campaign known as the Free Airing of Views; it was also called the Hundred Flowers Campaign. Mao Tse-tung proclaimed that one hundred schools of thought would bloom. The Communists promised that no labels would be affixed to those who offered their views, that no one would seize on their mistakes, and that no one would come down on them with a big stick. Through an intermediary, Bishop Tang asked the government to be lenient with the priests who had served part of their sentence and to release them. This became the basis for the charge against him that he asked the government to release the counterrevolutionaries.

For twenty-two monotonous years, Bishop Tang was mostly alone but sometimes in the company of others. He took cold baths to strengthen his body and his will, he kept all the regulations that did not conflict with his principles of faith, and he treated the wardens as his superiors. He kept his cell clean by sweeping it thoroughly and making sure that the toilet bucket was always emptied. Along with hunger, he suffered from violent headaches. Spiritually, he keenly felt his isolation and was aware that he was being tested. In fact, he recognized that under the circumstances it was difficult to believe in God, but he persevered in prayer, and whenever he had the chance, he would look through a small window to catch a glimpse of a tall eucalyptus tree. Year after year, he observed the changing seasons; he was sensitive to the setting sun and the chirping of birds. Certainly God was giving him the grace to keep his faith. Consolation came in the knowledge that Catholics everywhere, the Jesuits especially, supported him in his prayers.

In his humbled position, Father Wong, priest and victim for Christ's sake, would also find himself closer to the Lord.

✥   ✥   ✥

ONE OF THE first things I should say about the prison is that it was generally spic-and-span. I had arrived with adequate clothing; those who hadn't were issued clothes. During the first six months, I was kept busy enough with the interrogations; it would be seven years before I was sentenced. From 1955 until 1960, I remained at Railway Station Jail; in 1960, I was transferred to a prison in what had been the French concession where I would spend the next two years. During these seven years, I would find myself sometimes in solitary confinement, sometimes sharing a cell with one other prisoner or a few others, and sometimes one of a crowd packed uncomfortably into a tiny space.

In those first days of prison life, sharing the cell with the telegraph operator offered a special grace. The telegraph operator told me that he had worked for the Kuomintang and asked about my case. "Well, I am a priest," I volunteered. He requested baptism. We were not supposed to talk in the cell, but over a period of time I communicated to him by writing the Our Father, the Hail Mary, and the Creed on the closed cell door using a wet rag. There wasn't much I could do in the way of explanation, but I did manage to say the words to him, which he repeated. He understood that the Hail Mary was a kind of greeting. The main thing was that his heart was pure and he was eager and open to learning about the faith; he was not like someone who didn't care about religion. Later on, another cell mate requested baptism. This one had been educated by the Salesians, so he was familiar with the prayers. He wanted to be baptized on his birthday—we had no trouble keeping track of the days because each time we handed in a deposition, we had to sign and date it—so, after seven days of preparation, I had him fall in behind me in the circle of prisoners walking in the outdoor shower. With water sprinkled over my shoulder, he was baptized in the name of the Father, the Son, and the Holy Spirit.

That prison where I spent the first five years was a busy place, especially in 1957 when there was a major crackdown on dissidence. Mao Tse-tung had invited people to speak freely and to criticize the government openly in what was known as the Hundred Flowers Campaign. But when they did, they were thrown into jail. There were intellectuals and peasants, professors and students. At one point we had eight men in the same cell, but then, after a roundup of dissidents, there were fifteen of us. The following night our number increased to twenty-three. With a crowd like that there was little sleeping space. The only workable solution was to have one man lie on the floor with his head in one direction, and the next man with his head in the opposite direction, and so on. If you got up, somehow your sleeping place disappeared. In the crowded cell, conditions were not very hygienic, and lice became a problem, especially among those who would eat hot rice and then perspire in their clothing, which remained unchanged day after day, night after night.

During one interrogation session, I was ordered to denounce the Legion of Mary. A cell mate had reported that he overheard me one night whispering the Hail Mary. Our Lady holds a special place in my heart, so much so that I refer to her not simply as Mary, but rather as Our Lady or Blessed Mother, except when saying the Hail Mary. On that occasion, my reference to Mary was misunderstood as my being connected with the Legion of Mary, though I was not a member. My refusal to denounce the Legion of Mary resulted in my hands being manacled behind my back, and I was returned to the crowded cell, where everyone seemed quietly embarrassed. The man who had made the report was in tears, so great was his sorrow.

One intent of the punishment was to humiliate by making the prisoner helpless to take care of ordinary bodily needs, but others helped me. The man who had reported me came to my aid, and a young man whom I had taught English fed me and sponged me at bath time during that hot and muggy summer. However, sleeping was rather uncomfortable and, in fact, downright painful. Apparently one night, when my stirring caused the chain to tighten, I cried out, "Jesus! Jesus!" Still, I remembered the suffering of Our Lord and was not tempted to give in. When approached again about denouncing the Legion of Mary, I stated that it was a religious organization, not a political organization. The agent who ordered the handcuffs didn't understand that; all he knew was that his job was to break up the Legion of Mary. Putting the handcuffs on was his business.

The handcuffs were finally removed after fifty days, and I was grati-
fied once again by the insight of John Henry Newman; perhaps my
stubbornness was painful for me, but it worked in God's favor. *Ad
Majorem Dei Gloriam,* to the Greater Glory of God! And then my
thoughts were of Gladys, who, I knew, was praying for me, for the
Sisters of Social Service have a special devotion to the Holy Spirit. I
made the connection between my fifty days and nights in handcuffs
and the fifty days and nights between Easter and Pentecost, which
marks the descent of the Holy Spirit on the apostles. I felt blessed.

I recalled the reflection that I had made that night of September 26,
1955, as I was ordered to lower my head, first in the car on the way to
prison and then again as I was led inside the building. It occurred to
me that this kind of humility provided an extraordinary grace,
empowering me as both a priest and a victim. By ordination I was a
priest, and now, as a victim on the side of truth and justice, I was
closer to Our Lord. My prison ministry was not necessarily about
baptizing people or even preaching to them through words. In fact, I
didn't consider my command of the Chinese language sufficient to
demonstrate the right reasoning required for instruction that the
Chinese would expect in a sermon; they would label my preaching as
meiyou daoli, that is, lacking in instruction. But I could preach by
suffering in silence; it was a way to touch the hearts of those around
me and encourage them. I think that the Communists unwittingly
gave us priests, by separating us, the opportunity to touch many
hearts in our different entourages. Once again, *Ad Majorem Dei
Gloriam!*

❖ 12 ❖

Prayer in Prison

*F*ATHER WONG'S PRAYER *life, grounded in Ignatian spirituality, was enriched by his Chinese heritage. The Spiritual Exercises of St. Ignatius begin with the Presupposition, which would have one place a good interpretation on a neighbor's statement, taking it as sincere. For Father Wong, sincerity in seeking God is the key to salvation, superseding any profession of faith; he has a special fondness for the Eucharistic prayer that asks God to remember all those who seek him with a sincere heart. Confucian teachings refer to the sincerity of the individual in making sacrifices on behalf of their ancestors, and Confucius's pupil Tseng Tze wrote that sincerity rectifies the mind of the individual so that personal life can be cultivated. The cultivation of personal life leads to the family's being regulated, and when the family is regulated, the state is in order. When the state is in order, there can be peace in the world.*

Early in the Exercises, Ignatius offers the call to indifference, or to detachment, as it is sometimes better translated. Raised in a Buddhist household, Father Wong had an appreciation for the idea that suffering is brought on by desire and strife and that freedom comes from indifference. Buddhist scriptures recount that the perfect way knows no difficulties; it simply refuses to make preferences. Ignatius, too, aims for detachment from all created things so that one does not seek health rather than sickness, wealth rather than poverty, honor rather than dishonor, or a long life rather than a short one.

Also early on in the Exercises comes the use of the imagination to sense evil in the world to the point of seeing fire, hearing shrieking, feeling pain, tasting bitterness, and smelling suffering. Father Wong was able to take the opposite view as well and know that what God had created was good—the saints, the heavens, the sun, the moon, the stars, the elements, the fruits, the birds, fishes, and animals. Perhaps an unconscious recalling of his first calligraphy lesson expressing the teaching of Mencius, "Man, at the beginning, seeks goodness," enhanced his understanding of the call of Ignatius to seek the glory of God.

Central to Father Wong's prayer life in prison was the examen of Conscience, which he practiced daily and with great sincerity. Prescinding from the Christian conviction that we need God's grace to advance in the way of Christlike virtue, we observe that the ultimate concern of Confucius was to attain the highest possible level of human perfection. This involves continuous learning, an ever-deepening personal knowledge about being human on a personal, existential level. It means renovating oneself each day and continuing to do so day after day. Ignatius, promoting daily renewal, makes the examen the one prayer never to be preempted, even when one is busy carrying out God's work.

Although in prison there was little apparent opportunity to commit sin, Father Wong and Bishop Tsang sought divine guidance in growing more tolerant, in dealing with unbelief, and in accepting love. St. Thomas Aquinas, affirming that one is bound to love God with the whole heart, suggested that one progresses toward this goal by tending toward love. Tending toward love is what Father Provincial had in mind when his only advice to the George Wong upon his arrival at the Novitiate was to be generous. Even in prison Father Wong would continue to grow in generosity.

Father Wong always practiced the examen before lunch, thanking God for providing sustenance as he took in the aroma of the meager meal being delivered. Mao's Great Leap Forward in 1958, designed to transform China overnight from a poor agricultural country to a modern industrial nation by putting peasants to work in small-scale factories, resulted in failure and a nationwide famine. In prison there were sometimes so few grains of rice that Father Wong could see his reflection in the tin cup before he started to eat, and yet he tells us that he never suffered from hunger.

Confucius, in speaking about how self-knowledge transformed his life into a meaningful existence, once described himself as a person so engaged in the vigorous pursuit of learning that he forgot his food and so happy to forget his worries that he was not aware of old age coming on. Sts. Francis and Clare, when sitting down to eat, were rapt in God by the overabundance of divine grace descending on them. Refreshed by spiritual food, they paid little attention to material food. Father Wong was neither engaged in a fascinating intellectual pursuit nor face to face with a friend as Francis of Assisi was with Clare, and yet, always in the presence of God and Our Lady, he was indeed rapt in divine grace.

Indifference actually protected him from the so-called sweet-and-sour treatment of the prison authorities, who would alternate between kindness and cruelty to the prisoners as a means of confusing and weakening them. Not consciously on guard about brainwashing, Father Wong simply accepted the handcuffs, refusing all offers to have them removed if he denounced the Legion of Mary. He had no quarrel with the government official who, he reasoned, was simply carrying out his duty. He accepted the loving ministrations of his cell mates but ignored the guards' offers of superfluous food.

❖   ❖   ❖

A NOTHER GRACE WAS the growing awareness, not just of Christ's presence, but of the connection between his presence and the emptiness of victimhood. This wasn't some immediate epiphany but a gradual development related to the Suscipe, the prayer St. Ignatius proposes in the "Contemplation for Obtaining Divine Love" in the book of the Spiritual Exercises:

> Take, Lord, and receive all my liberty,
>> my memory, my understanding, and my entire will,
>
> All that I have and call my own.
> Whatever I have or hold, you have given to me.
> I restore it all to you and surrender it wholly
>> to be governed by your will.
>
> Give me only your love and your grace
>> and I am rich enough to ask for nothing more.
>
> Amen.

It is a prayer not just to be said but to be lived in all its richness and fullness. Ignatius talked about less being more, and he was right.

Christ was ever present, and time did not matter. Still, without a watch I found the rays of sunlight coming through the window both a marvelous grace and a practical way to mark the hours as they moved from one point to the next in the room. Besides knowing the date from the signing of depositions those first months, I was able during the entire time in prison to keep up with the seasons by reading the newspaper, something that was encouraged since the publications were basically propaganda. Events were reported and proved interesting.

Over the years, I followed what was going on in the Suez Canal, John F. Kennedy's showdown with the Russians regarding Cuba, Henry Kissinger's diplomacy, and Richard Nixon's visit to China. Nixon's visit was presented as a sign of America's weakness, since the so-called Paper Tiger made no demands on China, such as a change in its policy regarding Taiwan, in contrast to China's refusal to deal with the Vatican as long as the Vatican maintained relations with Taiwan.

I also kept up with Advent and Christmas, Lent and Easter, and in doing so, I was praying with Father Frank and with Gladys and with the entire universal church. I keenly knew that they—individuals, my Jesuit brothers, and congregations—were praying for me. There were times when I was in solitary confinement—including once as a punishment for writing a note to a fellow prisoner—but I was in the presence of God and Our Lady. Little did the Communists understand that I was never alone.

Although circumstances dictated some variations, my daily prayers, always said privately and in silence, were basically the same. When in a group cell, we exercised at a prescribed time by walking one after the other in a circle in silence. What a glorious opportunity for meditation and reflection! I was able to make my Ignatian retreat, redoing the Spiritual Exercises with particular emphasis on the public life of Jesus. The point of the Second Week is to know Jesus more clearly, love him more dearly, and follow him more nearly; prison provided an excellent setting for contemplating his life and teachings.

In fact, I fashioned a rosary out of a rag, putting five knots in a string to represent half a decade. I usually said four rosaries a day—each time including the Joyful Mysteries, the Sorrowful Mysteries, and the Glorious Mysteries, with my own Public-Life-of-Jesus Mysteries inserted between the Joyful Mysteries and the Sorrowful Mysteries. These began with the baptism of Our Lord followed by the forty days and nights in the desert that were a preparation for his ministry. The second mystery of his public life was the choosing of his disciples, and the third the Sermon on the Mount from St. Matthew's Gospel. The fourth mystery was the founding of the church, with St. Peter as the rock, and meditating on this point provided an intense consolation; even in isolation I felt connected to the church, which Christ entrusted to Peter so that his work would be carried on. I concluded with the fifth mystery, which centered on the miracles. Traditionally, the rosary is based on three parts just as the Creed treats the Father, the Son, and the Holy Spirit. While the Creed addresses the birth, death, and resurrection of Our Lord, it omits his public life.

Of course, I did not limit the Spiritual Exercises to the Second Week. Everything is based on the Principle and Foundation of the First Week: we are created to praise, reverence, and serve God, to use our resources wisely to this end, and to make ourselves indifferent to all created things. The Third Week, on the suffering and crucifixion of Our Lord, though appropriate for meditation at any season, was especially suitable during Lent. The Fourth Week never ceased to bring the hope of the resurrection. So throughout the year, year after year, I was reminded of the gifts that flow from indifference, of the call to imitate Our Lord and the peace that comes from walking with him more closely, of the grace of victimization in union with the crucified Christ, and of the hopeful joy of the living Christ.

An important component of Ignatian prayer is the daily Examen of Conscience. In the Novitiate we did the examen before lunch. We attached a little string of beads to our cassocks; the beads were placed at the top of the string. Whenever we had done something we were ashamed of, like speaking harshly to someone or not listening carefully, a bead was pulled down. Then during the examen each novice could reflect on his infractions. With God ever present, I decided to do my daily examen before lunch, which was announced not just by the position of the sun and shadows in the cell but also by the aroma coming from the meals as they were being distributed in the prison.

Doing the examen just before lunch was not simply a habit retained from the Novitiate. The first part is a prayer of thanksgiving. As the aroma of rice swept through the halls and reached my senses, it seemed right to give thanks to God. There were many things to be grateful for: the gift of faith, the friendship and prayers of Father Frank and Uncle Ed and Sister Candida, membership in the universal church, my memory, my vocation, the everlasting presence of God, and peace, joy, and hope in the knowledge that all things work for the good for those who love Our Lord. I was also thankful for little consolations that would come through the kindness of other prisoners.

The second part of the examen is to ask God for light, for the grace to recognize my transgressions, which I would seek to identify even though there wasn't much I could do locked in a prison cell. But I was aware of my defects and of my need to grow. The third part of the examen is to make an account of the thoughts, words, and deeds of the previous hours, and then, fourthly, to express sorrow for sins and ask for pardon. The fifth part is to pray for strength in order to make amends.

Today, instead of calling this exercise the Examen (or Examination) of Conscience, we say Examen of Consciousness, a term coined by George Aschenbrenner, S.J. I didn't think about the semantics while I was in prison, but I understand the nuance and think that what I was doing was not so much evaluating what I had done right or wrong but growing over the years in awareness of what moved me closer to God in thought, word, and deed. In fact, St. Ignatius did not limit the examen to the negative. He was interested in correcting faults, but he also recognized the positive by practicing virtues and cultivating the good. Just as Jesus advanced in wisdom, age, and grace before God and man, we seek to grow spiritually, something that requires consciousness, not just conscience.

After the examen, I had my meal of rice. Usually there wasn't much to eat; at times you could almost see your reflection at the bottom of the tin cup even before you had eaten. And the rice husks they fed us irritated my intestines to the point that in later years surgery was necessary. It wasn't much food, and I wouldn't have minded more, but it was adequate. I will say this: I never suffered from hunger.

✣ 13 ✣

A Christmas Memory

*I*GNATIUS KUNG PIN-MEI, *the first Chinese bishop of Shanghai, ordained Father Wong in 1951. He was arrested on September 8, 1955, and Father Wong's arrest followed. The newspaper account spoke of Bishop Kung and his counterrevolutionary group, that is, the priests of Shanghai. The Communists then engaged in a massive indoctrination program designed to teach the Catholics of Shanghai, who numbered about 150,000, that the arrest of their bishop was legitimate. Realizing that Catholic lay leaders also had a major influence on the faithful, the authorities launched a campaign to identify them, round them up, and isolate them. The government targeted the Legion of Mary as a subversive organization whose adherents referred to themselves, in military language, as legionnaires.*

Prior to the 1948 institution in China of the Legion of Mary, there existed an extensive Catholic Action Movement. Men and women catechists offered instruction, brought about genuine conversions as a result of their knowledge of the people they served, and were responsible for thousands of baptisms. Lo Pahong, the Shanghai businessman who requested that the California Jesuits come to China, was president of Catholic Action until his assassination in 1938. During the Sino-Japanese War, members of Catholic Action assisted priests and even took over the apostolate in places priests could not penetrate.

After the Communist takeover in 1949, the legionnaires were indispensable in carrying out the work of the church. One barrier that they had to overcome was the Chinese taboo against meetings with both genders present, a restriction that has since been removed by the Communists. In those days, however, mixed meetings were unheard of, and in the first public meeting the legionnaires were not comfortable; the young women especially were acutely embarrassed. However, after prayers were said and the real work was outlined, the change in atmosphere at that meeting marked the beginning of a movement where not only did clergy and laity work side by side but where men and women collaborated publicly and without shame.

Another obstacle was that Christians were not accustomed to mixing with non-Christians. This attitude was also to change as the legionnaires began seeking opportunities to mingle with potential catechumens. Some placed themselves at the entrances to churches to meet the non-Christians coming to Mass. In low voices, they instructed them about the Mass and explained the prayers. On a personal level, the legionnaires began frequent reception of the sacraments as they engaged in a more active prayer life. Apparently, their practices had a positive influence on attendance at Mass and in building stronger faith communities.

Some missionaries in the nineteenth and early twentieth centuries, aware that the family formed the backbone of political and social life in China, refused to accept individual converts out of fear that they might backslide. The conversion of whole lineages and entire villages resulted *in rural Catholics living in separate enclaves from non-Catholics. The resulting ghetto mentality would enable Catholics, as communities, to stand firm under Communist rule. The Legion of Mary, on the other hand, offered Chinese Catholics, as individuals, the opportunity to do the Lord's work. Catholics encountering one another in prison offered encouragement and support. Thanks to a simple carol hummed by one inmate, Christ was born for Father Wong on Christmas of 1962 in Ward Road Prison.*

✛   ✛   ✛

AFTER THE FIRST six months, my interrogations were over. With no respect for international law, the government let me wait seven years before a sentence was given; during this time I was not a convict but retained the status of one in custody. I had spent five years in the big custody house, that is, Railway Station Jail, and two years mainly in solitary confinement in the French concession prison. On the day of sentencing, I was handcuffed and taken in a jeep to an immense hall that had once been the Shanghai Municipal Court.

The hall was empty except for me and the two policemen at my side, facing a table behind which four judges were seated. The list of my crimes was read. Instead of specific crimes, mostly the names of other missionaries were cited; we were guilty of being counter-revolutionaries. I was also charged, not with belonging to the Legion of Mary, but with being a friend and accomplice of the Legion. My superior, Vincent Chu, the pastor at Christ the King, was given fourteen years in prison, and I was honored with a fifteen-year sentence. The first seven years in prison counted. The next eight were to be spent in *laogai,* or reform through labor.

Asked if I had anything to say, I replied, "Everything you accuse me of is connected with religion. There is supposed to be freedom of religion in China." Dismissed with an abrupt "Get out," I was taken—

in handcuffs now, as a convict—to Ward Road Prison, Shanghai's largest prison and perhaps the largest in the Far East. I was in my cell for only a short time before being told to gather my belongings, that is, my dictionary and a quilt, and then I was moved to a community cell where a wonderful surprise awaited: a reunion of priests!

For three glorious weeks in 1962, fourteen of us shared our lives together. The wardens did not even try to keep us quiet. There was much joyful excitement at being reunited. Interestingly, one priest from Peking took it upon himself to make estimates regarding the future of those in the room. When he got to me, he made some disparaging remark like, "Father Wong, he can't do anything." I found this attitude puzzling and rather presumptuous, but not preoccupying.

Rather, I was thrilled about the companion next to me, Father Shen Tseng Li, a diocesan priest who had been procurator for his diocese before he and his bishop, now Cardinal Kung, were arrested. Father Shen had a good reputation; I was aware that he was well liked by parishioners. He told me that he was interested in becoming a Jesuit, and so I exuberantly told him all about our novitiate and our Constitutions. I don't remember what predictions were made about him, but I can testify that he worked actively in Shanghai following prison and did remarkable things. Father Shen eventually did become a Jesuit; I received his vows in Shanghai. At the time of our joint incarceration, I can say that I recognized in him a kindred spirit.

Our group of priests was disbanded as we were separated and sent to serve our various sentences. Some of us had to wait before actually being sent to our camps. Not judged physically strong enough to work at the labor camp at that time, much less make the trip there, I was transferred to the municipal jail for six months of strengthening. Now that I had been sentenced, I was allowed to have visitors once a month. It really wasn't shameful to be visiting a convict, for the public knew that many were imprisoned for religious convictions and not for real crimes; in fact, there might have been a certain pride associated with the prison visits.

My sisters, my brother, my sister-in-law, and even my nephews came to visit. They didn't come all at the same time but separately, and they were permitted to bring gifts of food: sweets, apples, bananas, meat shreds. During the previous years I had never been sick, thank God, my annual infirmary visits having been for routine checkups for communicable diseases like tuberculosis. Now I was experiencing six months of better treatment that included monthly visits with my family and more food. The small weekly ration of meat remained the same, but my diet was supplemented by foodstuffs procured by my family thanks to subsidies from the California Jesuits.

The cadres at the prison marked Christmas Day by offering the Christians a piece of pork. There were a couple of ironies surrounding this gesture, which was a weak attempt to demonstrate that we were in prison not because of religion but because we were counterrevolutionaries. For one thing, my cell mate did not enjoy the same privilege. Secondly, a Catholic priest would have preferred being able to celebrate Mass, to read the Bible, and to sing carols. Praying openly was, of course, taboo, and so I privately said my prayers and my dry Mass as I did daily, dispensing with the species and with certain rubrics.

The first Christmas in prison, I managed to say three dry Masses, thanking God for my memory of the Latin words and then meditating with joy on these three Masses of the birth of Our Lord. I could hear angelic choirs singing "Glory to God in the Highest" in my prison cell and in the depths of my heart and soul. That first Christmas was during my period of interrogation; another gift that would have been more valuable than the piece of pork would have been the canceling of the interrogation for that day. But my number, One Three Two Seven, was called, and so off I went for the exasperating business of grilling and more grilling. However, the inquisitor grinned at me and asked me if I had enjoyed my brunch. Then I was dismissed in what appeared to be a win-win arrangement in the midst of bureaucratic formality. It was his duty to show up for work, and so he did. Now we were both free to get on with our respective business for the day.

While in the city jail where I was sent to build up my strength before being dispatched to the labor camp, I had a very joyous holiday as I was able to celebrate my forty-fourth birthday (according to the lunar calendar) on Christmas (according to the Western calendar). Another happy coincidence was that the observance of the Nativity happened to be the monthly visiting day, so I was able to see my people again and receive their gifts of personal items and food.

Something else special had happened that week. I met a French prisoner during the morning walk taking place on the rooftop, five stories up. Recognizing me as the priest who said Mass in our parish church, he kindly offered to lend me his books: Oscar Wilde's *The Picture of Dorian Gray* and Pascal's *Pensées.* There was a bonus with the latter as it contained Advent meditations. I felt so grateful to my new friend that I wrote him a letter of thanks. Unfortunately, as I was writing, the warden passed by and saw me through the iron grill. Immediately he confiscated my letter and the books, interrogating me about my relationship with the French prisoner. He searched all my belongings but did not take the apples and cookies my family had brought me (although the two young scamps thrown into my cell a couple of days later would manage to consume the treats).

Of course, I was deeply saddened that the books were taken and that I was cut off from my friend; it was one of my most depressing moments. But that night, after a far-from-sumptuous meal, my ears caught the strains of "Minuit chrétiens," or "O Holy Night," sung soulfully by the Frenchman. What a wonderful consolation! Christ was born for me that night in prison!

✣ 14 ✣

Laogai

In 1960, Harry Wu, *a university student who was never formally tried or charged, was sent to a* laogai *camp. During his nineteen years in the* laogai *system he suffered torture and would have died of hunger had it not been for the weeds he found in the fields and the frogs and snakes he captured in irrigation ditches. He witnessed the deaths of fellow prisoners due to disease and starvation. The Great Leap Forward had been a disaster, producing one of the greatest famines in Chinese history.*

Many Catholics, including thousands of laypeople, joined multitudes of strangers in the labor camps. Theoretically, the camps were designed to change the thinking and attitudes of criminal and political prisoners who were to be returned to society as productive contributors to their respective communities. Large-scale transfers of prisoners, sometimes crowded for days into filthy railway cars of slow-moving trains, occurred according to the demands of the various manufacturing units.

Completion of a sentence did not result in release; inmates could be retained as workers. Actually, not only prisoners were shipped off to these camps; teenagers, some enthusiastically volunteering and some without the consent of their families with whom they would have no contact for years, were transported to faraway farms, plantations, mines, and factories where they provided unpaid labor. Just as important as the reeducation role of the labor camps was the economic role. Laborers farmed, built roads, opened mines, made bricks, operated looms, knitted socks, and manufactured screws.

The daily schedule usually consisted of ten or more hours of work with two hours for indoctrination sessions. Every two weeks there might be a break day. Some reports describe the farm prisons as worse than the industrial camps. Farm facilities were primitive, and the labor was backbreaking. One priest felt fortunate to be sent to a tool factory instead of to a farm. He claimed that anyone with a sentence of more than twelve years of labor would not be directed to a farm because, on the farm, the person would expire before the sentence did.

On his journey to White Lake Farm, Father Wong passed through a village and spent the night in a building that had been a Catholic church. During the land reform of the 1950s, churches in rural areas were closed, and church property was requisitioned by the government. Some church buildings were razed. Farming families in many regions gathered for prayer in large dugouts, passing their faith from one generation to the next. Father Wong, that night in the former church, took comfort in knowing that Our Lord had once resided in the tabernacle.

❖   ❖   ❖

L AOGAI IS USUALLY translated as "reform through labor." *Lao* means "work," and *gai* refers to changing one's mind. My experiential translation might be "brainwashing through work." The famous dissident Harry Wu, born to a privileged family in 1937, was both educated and baptized at St. Francis Xavier College in Shanghai. He was imprisoned and eventually sent to a *laogai* camp after expressing his honest point of view as a university student, even though he had been invited to do so and had been told that there would be no reprisals. After Mao died, he was released, eventually making it to the United States, where he declared himself the enemy of the *laogai* system. In 1995, Harry Wu returned to China against the advice of the U.S. government because he wanted to document the abuses of the *laogai* system. Of course, he was arrested. He became a bargaining chip that year when the United Nations Conference on Women was to be held in Beijing. He was expelled prior to Hillary Rodham Clinton's appearance at the conference. Many people rightfully associate the *laogai* system with Harry Wu.

I was shipped off to be reformed in such a system. My camp was called Bai Hu Nong Ch'ang, or White Lake Farm. Originally there was a lake there, but the Communists realized that the land was fertile so they pumped the water into the Yangtze River and planted rice. Actually, my understanding is that the enterprise was a losing proposition. There was very little profit to be made in selling rice to other countries, but the government needed a place to put prisoners. Whatever the case might have been, White Lake Farm was where I was headed in 1963.

The first part of the two-day trip to White Lake Farm was by bus from the prison to the railway station, and then by train to the river; we were always under armed guard. We spent the night in the countryside in a public auditorium that once had been a Catholic church. It was a spacious building with an elevated section where the altar had been. The benches were no longer there; we were supposed to sleep on the floor. Taking consolation in the thought that Our Lord had once lived in the tabernacle of this church, I lay down for the night in the choir loft, where I knew it would be quieter.

The next day the journey continued. Several hundred of us, including some of my fellow Jesuits, traveled by sampan, ten boats in all. I would estimate that there were one hundred men in each boat, so there were about one thousand men destined for White Lake Farm. I met another university student who, like Harry Wu, had been arrested as a rightist and sentenced to *laogai* after having responded to the invitation to speak out frankly during the Hundred Flowers Campaign. The message from the government was, "Shout all you can to express your opinion!" He got fifteen years for expressing his. It turned out that he and I would stay in touch; many years later he married and sent me a picture of his wife and family.

During the trip, it was difficult to talk at leisure. The boats, with huge, wide bottoms, were very crowded. You couldn't really stand or sit or move about. If you needed to pass water, you just did it. The trip was pretty uncomfortable; my body was cramped from years of inactivity. When we disembarked, our belongings—in my case, my clothes and bedding and my huge Chinese-English dictionary, which would be confiscated during the Cultural Revolution—were put into carts. We had a long walk to the camp; it was my first exercise in seven years apart from the half-hour walks in the cells or on the prison roof. Arriving at the camp, we were divided into units of two hundred men watched over by armed guards instructed to shoot anyone who tried to escape. That evening we had a dull, saltless meal of rice and carrots. The next day I ached so badly that I couldn't get up from bed.

My aching muscles resulted in a visit to the infirmary, which was a blessing in disguise because I met a Catholic doctor who interestingly enough now lives in the United States. First, he gave me some advice about using my aches and pains as a means for getting an easy job like a watchman's job. Second, he gave me some port wine in a penicillin bottle with a rubber stopper. The doctor also wanted to practice his English, but someone reported our conversation. The cadre reprimanded us, "You have broken the rules by speaking English." I was transferred to another unit where for two years I tended the vegetable garden.

Every month we were allowed to send a postcard home; there was a fifty-character limit on the message. I sent a card to my sister requesting some biscuits, the kind that I used to have before breakfast. She understood my hint, and soon I received a package containing not only vitamins, meat shreds, and dried fruit but also, and especially, the wafers that she had baked herself. With the wafers from home and the port wine from the doctor, I was all set. The memory of Father Frank's patristic-theology lecture on Polycarp lying in prison with the host on his chest was alive in my heart and mind. I presumed permission to celebrate Mass in secret. The Mass was an extraordinary luxury rather than a daily event. Once, when I unstopped the penicillin bottle, the perfume of the wine filled the warm, dark room. "What a lovely fragrance!" exclaimed the voice of a sleepy roommate. Caution was necessary.

It turned out to be easy enough to store my things. My monthly postal parcels from home came in wooden containers that would be coveted gifts to my companions. We each had a locked box for our belongings. Once a quarter there were inspections; sometimes they turned up things that a man had been hoarding, such as his clothes. At the camp we could request clothes. Those issued by the government were stamped *laogai*. Some men, perhaps with the intention of escaping in the clothes they had brought, since they did not have the *laogai* stamp, asked for new labor-camp-issued garments.

During one inspection, I prayed that the consecrated host in my box would not be disturbed. "Lord, please take care of Yourself. I have to take care of myself." The wine and the wafers were safe enough. On special feasts that Providence helped me remember, I would lie on my bed and say Mass, receiving Our Lord in union with the universal church. The celebration of the Eucharist was a deeply meaningful and powerful experience, larger than words and perhaps best left to silence, which is also a form of prayer.

✣ 15 ✣

Déjà Vu

*A*T WHITE LAKE *Farm, Father Wong would be involved in struggle*
sessions. A simple definition of the struggle session has it as a Chinese
invention combining intimidation, humiliation, and sheer exhaustion.
It has also been called an intellectual gang beating of one by many in
which not even the truth is a defense. Struggle sessions could go on for
hours or days or weeks with the victim being surrounded by peers who
criticized, insulted, and screamed at him or her. There might be slap-
ping, beating, and spitting. The goal was to get the target to confess,
whether or not a crime had been committed. Sometimes confessions
were scripted for the accused by the authorities, with cues for speaking
remorsefully and emotionally.

Prior to her arrest in 1958 when she was twenty-two years old,
Margaret Chu, the niece of Bishop Kung Pin-mei, was forced to attend
indoctrination sessions. Those who buckled under pressure and accepted

Communist tenets were allowed to return to their jobs and educational endeavors. Those who followed the church were dismissed from their jobs and denied university access. Concluding that to deny the pope was to deny Christ, Margaret prayed and meditated. She was sentenced to eight years in prison but would actually spend twenty-one years in various labor camps.

First, Margaret was sent to a transit facility where showers were available once a month to all prisoners except Catholics. Then she went to a camp where she worked eighteen hours a day in a knitting factory; later the workday was reduced to ten hours. The time allocated for daily reeducation exercises remained two hours. During struggle sessions when she was asked what her crime was, she replied that she had committed no crime and that she was in the camp because of her Catholic faith. In this manner, she identified herself to other Catholics who secretly united with her. During one struggle session, people jumped on Margaret, cut her hair, and tied her so that any movement of the hands was painful. Later the ropes were removed; she was handcuffed for one hundred days, during which she was sent to the fields to work. Looking for God in the extreme heat, she found refuge in malodorous barrels used for toilets. Occasionally some of her Catholic friends came to her secretly with a wet towel to clean her face and rub her back. Others apologized for having criticized her, claiming that they had been under pressure to do so.

After her sentence was up, Margaret had a bit more freedom as a worker in her labor camp. In 1974, she got to know Ignatius Chu. Seven of Ignatius's brothers were in labor camps because of their faith. The eighth brother, Jesuit Michael Chu, was out of the country at the time of the Communist takeover. With secret plans to marry, on the designated day Margaret faked illness but did not go to the clinic. Instead, she managed to get to the train station, where she and Ignatius were greeted by Ignatius's eldest brother, Jesuit Francis Chu. In a noisy restaurant, he offered a secret Mass with soda crackers and a few drops of wine, and they exchanged their marriage vows before God. Then, after taking Father Francis back to the train station, she and Ignatius returned to their respective dormitories. Ignatius and Margaret were able to join her brother Joe in the United States in 1980. After his second arrest, Father Francis died in prison in 1983 at the age of seventy. He had spent a total of thirty years as a prisoner.

Father Wong was accused of idealism in his laogai *struggle sessions.*

❖   ❖   ❖

IN THE HOT weather we were expected to work outside, but in the freezing cold weather, there was little we could do on the farm. So we had indoctrination classes and struggle sessions. Earlier, in describing *lapidatio,* the Saturday-night corrections at the Novitiate, I mentioned that some people might be tempted to compare them to the struggle sessions of the Communist regime in China. I also said that there was a major difference. In the case of the former, there was a sincere effort to help one's companion become the best that he could. We were young men then. Whether we realized it or not, we were not seeking to make everyone behave and think the same way; conformity wasn't the goal. What we were seeking was to help each other, in a supportive environment, to recognize our shortcomings so that we could improve on them. Perhaps our other nickname for the event, charity ball, was the more suitable.

The struggle sessions, on the other hand, were more like stone-throwing events that could with justification be called *lapidatio.* People were put on the hot seat in the center of the room, and others were encouraged to point out the faults in their behavior and thinking. I was accused of idealism, that is, of not being realistic, for saying that religion was above politics. I had no quarrel with patriotism, for our religion calls us to give the government its due. I don't think love for God and love for country are mutually exclusive. But in that society, religion had no place.

I don't have personal horror stories to report about being physically attacked, although there was the threat of handcuffs if I didn't change my thinking. Others, more openly rebellious than I, were actually tortured. To get one of my fellow workers to confess his so-called wrongful thinking, they strung him from a rope and left him dangling for hours. Finally, he fell off, but he became loonylike. Some men died from harsh treatment while others starved in these camps, although starvation was not intended as a punishment. In the later years, the government stepped in and said that the treatment should be humane, that no punishment should be more than a prisoner could stand. What they were afraid of was that word about the actual conditions would get out through the likes of Harry Wu.

It was decided that my brain needed more washing through more labor, so I was transferred from the vegetable garden to the rice fields: planting rice, harvesting rice, planting rice. Perhaps the grape picking at the Novitiate prepared me in a minor way; there we were not allowed to speak English either, except for spiritual direction. However, in the rice fields, there was no benevolent father following us around inquiring about our spiritual life.

Rising at six, I was in the fields before seven and worked until nine at night, returning to my unit for a quick meal before collapsing on my bed. The work in the hot sun was terrifically difficult and fatiguing. It was necessary to plant the seedlings in a straight line. I was too slow, so I was assigned to string pulling. The strings were pulled from one end of a field to the other in parallel lines, as guides for the planters who would follow. Then the strings would be gathered up to be used for a new line. You had to keep ahead of the planters, rushing and plopping along in the paddies. One of the problems was that the string was made from straw and would break easily, so in one of my fifty-word postcards, I asked my sister to send some nylon string. It proved to be strong and, of course, worked much more satisfactorily.

I was praised for taking the initiative to procure the string, and that at the expense of my family. There were forms of public praise, but these compliments were of no interest to me.

Leeches attacked my legs in the rice paddies, and at least once every year I seemed to pass out from sunstroke. Luckily, there was a doctor in the camp who revived me and gave me injections. Then I was allowed to rest for a day. One time the doctor was afraid that I wouldn't survive. With my constitution I should have taken frequent breaks instead of working for so long a time at one stretch, but that kind of self-pacing wasn't allowed. Still, while life was tough and annoyances were plentiful, I think that the authorities in the camp were careful not to give us more than we could handle and were as attentive as they could be to matters of health.

There was a time when I was being treated for jaundice that my abdomen seemed to catch fire. The doctor at the infirmary didn't think it was serious, but when the surgeon saw me, he insisted that my appendix come out right then and there. Acupuncture was administered, but as those who attempted it were just amateurs, it had no anesthetizing effect. I was writhing in pain, and my arms and legs were eventually tied down to keep me from thrashing about. I did not suffer silently but screamed as the surgeon's knife cut into me. Actually, I was lucky, for without his intervention, my appendix would surely have ruptured. And there was another bit of good luck: I didn't suffer any aftereffects from anesthesia!

Every two weeks we had a day off to rest, wash, and mend our clothes and bedding. We weren't supposed to meet with our friends, but the Jesuits and other priests spread throughout the fifteen units in the camp managed to get together, though only in discreet pairs, on these holidays. Meeting in larger groups would have caught the attention of the guards, soldiers in the People's Army, who patrolled the place with guns in hand. Sometimes I would see Shen Tseng Li or Francis Wang or Yen Yun Liang or one of the Chu brothers. News, passed from one Jesuit to another, circulated among us; that was how

I first heard about Vatican II and the change from the Mass in Latin to the vernacular. For the time being, we each continued our private Masses in Latin, however. Together we mourned Pope John XXIII and put ourselves at the service of Paul VI. One thing that escaped our attention was the moon landing by the Americans in 1969. It was another fifteen years before that news circulated in China.

In July of 1969, the Yangtze River was overflowing, and there was a terrible flood at the farm. The two hundred men in our unit were joined for one month on top of a dike by one hundred more men from other units. Our only task was to carry dirt to build up the dike. We slept under a tent made of plastic, and each day we had about fifteen pounds of cabbage to mix in the rice that we shared among the three hundred of us. I was lucky to have some meat shreds with me as well as garlic; garlic helps relieve constipation.

During the Cultural Revolution, we were treated to movies about once a month. I am using the verb *treated* facetiously. The movies, the brainchild of Mao's wife Jiang Qing, were pure propaganda with no redemptive artistic quality. We were literally a captive audience, but even those not detained in prisons or camps were subject to this form of attempted brainwashing; factory workers were forced to buy cinema tickets to see the movies we saw for free. At White Lake Farm, before we had electricity, we used a generator to run the movie projector. When we got electricity, showing the film was easier.

I have already mentioned the monthly postal parcels that came from my family. These wooden crates brought tangible things that provided nourishment for my body and my soul. I credit the vitamins and the dried meat, fruit, and cookies with helping me survive. The wafers from my sister, the bread from the earth that human hands had made, became the bread of life, keeping me in touch with Reality with a capital *R*. One member of my unit, probably jealous of my good fortune, pointed out his suspicions about my family's not being able to afford to send me regular packages. The cadres paid no attention to his suspicions, but the fact is that the California Jesuits sent funds to a cousin of mine in Hong Kong who was able to send a money order to my brother in Shanghai. Along with all the tangible benefits, the support of my brother Jesuits carried an immeasurable spiritual consolation. Their love was deeply moving and gloriously empowering; indeed, I was a very rich man.

✣ 16 ✣

Home Leave

MAO TSE-TUNG *mobilized Chinese peasants who, enticed by songs and slogans that appealed to their idealism, made the Long March between 1934 and 1935. Although more than half the marchers died, the Chinese Communist Party proved itself the worthy opponent of the corrupt Kuomintang. During the Sino-Japanese War, Mao distinguished himself as a great leader. Key events in China since the Communist takeover in 1949 (known to the Chinese as the Liberation), include the land reform movement of the 1950s, the Hundred Flowers Campaign in 1956, the Great Leap Forward in 1958, and the Cultural Revolution that lasted from 1966 until the death of Mao Tse-tung in 1976.*

One Maoist goal was to close the social and economic gap between urban and rural populations and between mental work and manual work; the strategy included purging China of old thoughts, old culture, old habits, and old customs. Intellectuals were arrested and sent to labor camps or assigned jobs like sweeping streets and cleaning toilets. Those from the country were not issued permits to live in the cities, but urban adolescents were sent to work in rural areas. Classrooms were closed between 1966 and 1969, and universities did not reopen until the early seventies. Young people were incited to rebel against bourgeois authority by criticizing, humiliating, and persecuting their teachers. Recruited as Red Guards, adolescents destroyed books and works of art. It was at the beginning of the Cultural Revolution that Father Wong's Chinese-English dictionary was confiscated.

With an intent to break down family loyalties, government officials and neighborhood party leaders punished those related to intellectuals or to those identified as enemies of the people. There was no consistent definition as to what thoughts or crimes might characterize an enemy of the people. Singing old songs was a crime, for example, whereas revolutionary music was tolerated. For some, it was possible to escape persecution for the alleged sins of relatives by denouncing them and cutting off all contact with them.

Coinciding with Richard Nixon's 1972 visit to China, an attempt to develop revolutionary music, ballet, opera, literature, and films was launched under the patronage of Mao's third wife, Jiang Qing, a former movie actress. However, artists and writers, having witnessed the Hundred Flowers Campaign during which people were promised that there would be no sanctions if they spoke out frankly, were hesitant to express themselves freely. Two months after Mao's death in 1976, Jiang Qing was arrested as part of the Gang of Four; in 1981 she was convicted for her crimes. Under the leadership of Deng Xiaoping, the Communist Party officially condemned the Cultural Revolution.

❖ ❖ ❖

EIGHT YEARS AT White Lake Farm, combined with seven years in prison in Shanghai, should have marked the end of my incarceration in 1970. That is not the way it worked, though. What happened is that my status was changed from prisoner to worker or farmer. I was now eligible for an annual two-week home leave as well as a small wage beyond room and board, clothes, and medical care. Eventually, I would be reclassified as retired and qualify for a modest pension. In my retirement years, I would be able to write letters and then walk to the village to mail them. But I was not a free man. Coupons were required to buy food and clothes, and residency permits were necessary to live in another place. Whether *laogai* prisoner, worker, or pensioner, we had no residency permits allowing us to live elsewhere or coupons allowing us to buy what we needed.

Entitled to home leave, those farm workers deemed more diligent were in a priority category. I was in the other category, lagging behind, but my boss could see that I was doing my best in pulling those strings as I splashed through the muddy, leech-infested paddies. Rice flourishes in a hot climate, and we had two harvests, one in the spring or summer and the other in the autumn. And so, after lots of hard work, I was finally granted a home leave in 1972, the year of Nixon's visit to China. That same year Bishop James Walsh was released from prison and returned to the United States as a gesture of friendship. A Maryknoll father and the last foreign bishop in China, he was arrested in 1958. Though we did not come into face-to-face contact as prisoners, I remember hearing his voice once in the Railway Station Jail in Shanghai. And so that year he was off to the United States, and I, for the first time in seventeen years, after a long trip on foot to the village and then by bus to the station and then by train to Shanghai and then again on foot from the station, found myself at the doorstep of my family's house.

My two elder sisters lived there with my brother and sister-in-law and nephews. I know one priest who, on leave from labor camp, arrived at his family's home at about four in the morning. He waited outside until the sun came up because he didn't want to frighten his mother. In my case, everyone was roused out of bed early in the morning, but my sisters and brother hardly recognized me. My skin was black from the sun, and my fingernails and toenails had been dyed by the muddy water. On top of that, I was toothless. When I was first arrested I had partial dentures, but over the years my teeth dropped out one by one from the inadequate diet. At White Lake Farm, our rations depended on the category of work we were doing, and then there was a special regime of wet rice and cheese for toothless people like me. Once again in Shanghai, I was glad to be with my family and also glad that my mother had passed away in 1953; she had been spared the agony of my imprisonment, and now she didn't have to be startled by my appearance.

Shanghai was drab. There was no excitement or character in the streets; shops were dull and uninviting. Signs were colorless labels without any artistic quality. I ventured into a cinema to watch a film that was like those at the labor camp, pure and simple propaganda. My sister-in-law, wearing her Mao jacket, took me to a restaurant one day. All the people more or less blended together in a blue sea of Mao jackets. It was hard to recognize any spirit or personality. We never talked about it, but I noticed that my sister-in-law's Mao jacket never quite covered up the floral-print blouse she was wearing. The blouse, somehow a tad longer than the jacket, may have been her best chance of keeping a bouquet in the lifeless city.

One thing I was able to do in Shanghai was get a set of dentures. During my preprison days I had a very good Cantonese dentist. He and his wife were fervent Protestants, reading the Bible together every day and singing sacred hymns. They were present at my ordination. But they were no longer in Shanghai; actually they ended up in Los Angeles, where they died a few years ago. I tried in vain to locate a government dentist who could provide me with dentures in a short time. The next step was to look for a private dentist, though private dentists always lived with the threat of having the government confiscate their apparatus. As it happened, my brother and I met up with some friends in the street who directed me to an excellent underground dentist. His electric drill had been taken by the government, so he used a hand drill. He took an impression of my gums and within three days, just in time for my return to the *laogai* camp, he gave me a perfect set of false teeth.

At home, I was able to say Mass for my family and friends, and there were invitations to say Mass in the homes of others. My shaving cup, which I had acquired in the debris of a fire at St. Francis Xavier College many years before, was still at home. It served as a humble chalice in our catacomb-style meetings during the home leave of 1972 and again during the home leave of 1973. Technically, there was freedom of religion in China, and celebration of the Mass in private homes was permitted. But one of the strings attached to this privilege was that the home could only be your own. Sadly, there were renegade Catholics who, like puppeteers, were willing to pull at those strings. I did not know that because of someone's reporting on me, I would pay a hefty price for saying Mass in another home. My next home leave should have been in 1974. It would be denied, but this time there was very little talk about counterrevolutionary activity. It seemed clear to everyone in my unit at the labor camp that I was being punished because of my religion.

During my home leave of 1979 I became sick and so was exempted from returning to White Lake Farm. When my health was better, I was eventually able to teach English at Shanghai University; it was a government institution with classes held in what once had been the Jesuit high school. My teacher wages were no different from my farmer wages, but I earned a little extra money by giving lessons privately. At a later time I would also be asked to teach history. It seemed that an American woman who had been recruited to teach a course in United States history showed up in Shanghai with a trunkload of books. However, the books were being held at the customs house. A quick evaluation determined that many of them were worthy of

censure. The American teacher asked the headmaster to send someone to the customs house to fetch the books, but he refused to cooperate, claiming that they were her business. Disgusted, she left, and I
filled the vacancy.

Now, I had never studied American history, and there were no
textbooks, just mimeographed materials. The headmaster claimed
that I could write my own textbook, which the authorities would
publish, but the truth is that when I prepared the beginning of a textbook, they were not ready to publish what I had developed. I went
ahead with the course by first teaching about Abraham Lincoln and
the Gettysburg Address. For an examination, I instructed the students—there were about 120 of them—to be prepared to write about
the statement "this nation, under God, shall have a new birth of freedom." The students knew that I was a priest, and they also were aware
that I had connections with Catholics at the American consulate.
Whenever possible, I did what I could to help them obtain visas for
the United States. In class, though it was risky, I made frequent refer-
ences to the Scriptures.

✥ 17 ✥

The Public Church

*D*URING THE KOREAN WAR *(1950–1953), the Communists required all organizations receiving foreign funding to register with the government. The Religious Affairs Division, later called the Religious Affairs Bureau, monitored all religious activity in China. Religious groups were to observe the Three Autonomies: to become independent, self-supporting, and self-propagating. Some Protestant groups, finding the Christian gospel compatible with outreach to the poor as manifested in the land reform movement, were supportive of Chinese Communism; they began preparing Christian churches in China to become independent from their foreign sponsors. At first, relations between the Catholic Church in China and the Vatican were tolerated, although the government's official stance required the churches to be independent.*

In early 1951, Catholics published a document condemning the independent churches as schismatic. The popular position was that separa-

tion from the Holy See was the same as separation from Christ. Moreover, Catholic bishops and the Communists differed on the interpretation of the Three Autonomies. Catholics considered that the establishment of an indigenous hierarchy fulfilled the requirement for self-government. They did not feel that financial support from other Catholics, whether Chinese or foreign, went against the goal of being self-supporting as long as they did not accept financial support with political strings attached. And as long as religious leaders, including foreign missionaries, acted in the interest of the Chinese Catholics rather than in the interests of foreigners, the bishops believed that they had met the requirement of self-propagation.

By September 1951, when the Vatican Internuncio, Antonio Riberi, was expelled from China, most Protestant missionaries had already withdrawn. The Catholic Church became the target of the Chinese Communists, and a campaign was launched to seek the support of Catholic families for government programs.

In 1954, the Communists began attaching an element of patriotism to the church reform. That same year, Pope Pius XII issued an encyclical encouraging Chinese Catholics to reject the independent-church movement. The bishops of China manifested their intolerance by refusing the sacraments to any priest or layperson who joined the Communist Party. The Communist reaction, in the years that followed, was to arrest the bishop of Shanghai, the bishop of Guangzhou, priests, other religious, seminarians, and laypeople. In 1957, the national Chinese Catholic Patriotic Association was established; members denounced the Vatican, and the local election of bishops began. However, during the Cultural Revolution (1966–1976), all overt religious activity ceased in China. Red Guards, usually teenagers given license to beat and torture Christians, confiscated and destroyed religious articles and literature.

After Mao's death in 1976, the complete ban on religious activities was abandoned for pragmatic reasons. There was even a certain degree of self-criticism by the government regarding the lack of religious freedom during the Cultural Revolution. Providing churches so believers could gather was put forth as a duty of the government even though the official position of the Communists remained that of atheism. By 1980, the Chinese Catholic Patriotic Association, comprised of people professing their love of their country and their church, was seeking ways in which Catholics could contribute to the modernization of China. The public church, also known colloquially as the patriotic church, continued under the control of the Communists with no visible link to the Vatican.

❖   ❖   ❖

THANKS TO A new open-door policy, I was able to correspond with my friends and Jesuit confrères in California. Some letters, always written prudently, went by regular mail, and others were transmitted via circuitous routes by friendly couriers. Sometimes news was conveyed by visitors who, having been under surveillance and subject to inspection upon leaving the mainland, were better off not carrying mail. During this period, the contribution sent to me by the California Jesuits reached me through a third party, a man called Harry, who was the friend and confidant of Father Ted McElroy in Hong Kong. In 1979, Harry managed to meet me in Shanghai. He reported back to Father McElroy, who talked to Father Charles McCarthy (then visiting Hong Kong), who wrote to Father Edward Murphy, the procurator in California, that I had been severely reprimanded when it became known outside the circle of loyal family and friends that I had been saying Mass.

Not expecting my family to attend daily Mass, I celebrated the Eucharist, the *unum necessarium* of my Jesuit life, in the privacy of my bedroom long before dawn, keeping the Blessed Sacrament hidden behind the head of my bed with a tiny electric bulb giving votive light beside it. Providence provided a special grace by placing several Chinese Marist brothers in a house in my neighborhood. It was easy enough for me to go there undetected to celebrate Mass for them and their frequent visitors from abroad. Some of these visitors had been teachers in Shanghai in the old days. Meanwhile, I continued to meet occasionally, though cautiously, with underground priests.

The government, unable to wipe out religion, had established an official church in 1957 while I was in prison. There was a subtle form of persecution in the setting up of the Chinese Catholic Patriotic Association, a lay organization under the sponsorship and control of the State Religious Bureau. As the bureau did not recognize the spiritual supremacy of the pope, there was a forced separation between the church and the religious jurisdiction of the Vatican. From then on, the churches that were legally open for religious services became subject to state-appointed bishops, some of whom were married and all of whom had to sever their allegiance to the Holy See. Prayers for the pope became taboo in Catholic churches, and the Hail, Holy Queen prayer after Mass was forbidden because of its mention of our "mourning and weeping in this vale of tears." The authorities reasoned that this allusion to sadness ran counter to the happiness that came from our living in a socialist country.

But even the public churches operated under the auspices of the Patriotic Association were closed during the Cultural Revolution between 1966 and 1976, with the exception of a solitary church left open in Peking for Sunday worship by foreign diplomatic expatriates. Openly, there was no trace of religion except empty churches transformed for various uses. The Jesuit St. Peter's in Shanghai had become a two-story clubhouse for workers, and the gothic Church of St. Ignatius was turned into a warehouse for storing preserved fruits. The faithful, forced underground, met in private homes for worship.

In the fall of 1976, the demise of Mao Tse-tung and the tragic failure of the so-called Cultural Revolution were followed by the downfall of the Gang of Four and the restoration of the new paramount leader, Deng Xiaoping. He rectified many of the errors of his predecessor Mao. For instance, many intellectuals sentenced to forced labor during the Hundred Flowers Campaign of 1956 were reinstated in their former jobs and positions. Many surviving priests were also released and allowed to return to their families and, in some cases, to function as priests in the public church.

Religion was given new life as churches and, later, seminaries, reopened under the auspices of the Patriotic Association. Especially conspicuous were the nomination and consecration of new government-appointed bishops, all carried out independently of Rome. An "autonomous" bishops' conference was established in Peking, subject to the control of the Bureau of Religious Affairs. The inevitable consequence of this form of unrealistic "freedom of religion" in China has been to lead many of the government-appointed bishops to establish, through sub-rosa channels, their own spiritual ties with Rome. Those caught in underground activities are severely punished.

Actually, the majority of Chinese Catholics did not join the Patriotic Association. In May of 1980, over ten thousand Catholic fishermen, descendants of converts from the eighteenth century, steered their boats to Zosé, the shrine to the Blessed Mother outside of Shanghai that is a national place of pilgrimage for Chinese Catholics. Traditionally, the fishermen and their ancestors had paid homage to Our Lady during the month of May, receiving blessings for their marriages and visiting the Blessed Sacrament.

Anticipating the renewal of this tradition in 1980 with the more open attitude toward religion, they instead found the shrine desecrated and the statues of the Stations of the Cross missing. Even the statue of Our Lady holding the Infant Jesus with his arms outstretched was gone. The fishermen forced their way into the closed basilica, lighting candles and spending long hours in prayer; some professed to have seen visions of Our Lady. The government's Bureau of Religious Affairs dispatched agents to the scene, but the fishermen would not let them interfere. However, photographs were taken, and those identified in the photographs were arrested and sent to prison.

The Zosé incident particularly angered the Communists. The following year, they restored the shrine, using the location for the official opening of the seminary of the public church. Another incident also incited the wrath of the Communist authorities. In 1980, the Jesuit bishop of Guangzhou, Dominic Tang, was released, frail and sickly, after twenty-two years in prison, having never renounced his allegiance to the pope. Initially, he was told that he would not be a bishop, but somehow the authorities let the Christians decide that they wanted him as bishop, and so his status was made official. Unlike members of the Protestant, Muslim, or Buddhist Patriotic Associations, Catholics were not given permission to travel outside the country, and yet Bishop Dominic Tang, though not a Patriotic, was allowed to travel to Hong Kong for medical treatment. After surgery for his cancer, he was well enough to travel to Rome where he was named archbishop of Guangzhou, which provoked a violent reaction in Peking.

Although I had managed to procure a visa from the American consulate in Peking and was offered a teaching position at Loyola High School in Los Angeles, I was not granted a passport. Several Jesuit fathers were arrested in 1981 for their participation in services at Zosé. Rather than being able to leave for California, I was ordered in November of that year to return to White Lake Farm.

Two respected Patriotic Catholics visited me in my home, urging me to forget the pope and join the independent movement. The conversation, kept cordial, continued for an hour, the implication being that the order to return to White Lake Farm might be rescinded if I would change my allegiance. We shook hands, but the Patriotics, as I called them, since the appellation "patriot" has a different meaning, understood that my response to their attractive offer was an inflexible "no, not for the world." I made a note in my diary: "An hour of hot air."

For the three previous years, I had been teaching not only at Shanghai University but also at the Foreign Language Institute. One of my assignments, a juicy plum in my view, was to create a series of English-language lessons on tape; this project, though never realized, aligned with the Four Modernizations—the post-Mao plan to make progress in agriculture, industry, science, and technology by the year 2000. I was able, however, to take great joy in the relations that developed from my private English lessons. Often I was able to help the families of my pupils get U.S. visas, since I could put a word in on their behalf with the Catholics at the consulate. But I wasn't able to help myself, probably because of my own naïveté. It did not occur to me to bribe the cadre by offering him money or the gift of a television set, although doing so would certainly have procured my passport, if not in 1980, then in later years.

Nevertheless, life had been pleasant enough with my family in Shanghai even though it was not always harmonious. Alice, in her old age, had her difficulties and didn't always get along with the others, especially our sister-in-law, Julie, who was really a good person. Willie had also suffered for his fidelity to Our Lord, but actually he would be complimented in his retirement for his public service, which he carried out by working as a street-crossing guard. Although Julie and both my sisters were excellent cooks, Rosie would retain her role as Madonna of the Kitchen for years to come. I particularly remember the delicious four-pound duck she braised to celebrate the January birthday of Father Frank though, of course, he could not taste it since he was in Los Gatos. The youngest members of the household were my grandnephew, little Iggie (K.K.), my grandniece, baby Mary, and my three nephews, Ignatius (or Iggie), Johnny, and Eddie. Eddie would accompany me back to White Lake Farm.

�֥ 18 ✣

Back on the Farm

*T*HE CHINESE GOVERNMENT, *aware that religion could not be sup-pressed, took measures after the Cultural Revolution to permit religion under the auspices of the Catholic Patriotic Association in the case of the Catholic faith. Associations were also created for Protestants, Muslims, Buddhists, and Taoists. The goal was for the government to control religion. Two incidents, already mentioned by Father Wong, dis-turbed the Chinese Communists: the visit of the fishermen and other pilgrims to the shrine at Zosé and the appointment by Pope John Paul II of Dominic Tang Yee-Ming, S.J., as archbishop of Guangzhou (Canton).*

After twenty-two years in prison without a trial or even a sentence, Bishop Tang was released from prison on June 9, 1980. To his surprise, reporters were present as the officer in charge returned his rosary to him. He was also given a sum, minus what the government felt was due for certain expenses, to compensate for the ruby of his episcopal ring, con-fiscated at the time of his arrest. Led to a meeting with members of the Chinese Catholic Patriotic Association and Protestant clergy, Bishop Tang listened to a speech about the great clemency of the government that had decided to release him. He signed the prepared release docu-ment stating that he had resisted the suppression of the Legion of Mary, that he had encouraged students to study during the Korean War instead of urging them to join the army and resist America, and that he had said it was not fair to confiscate the assets of capitalists since the government allowed private commercial enterprises to exist and to make profit. Moreover, he had requested the release of priests whom the government considered counterrevolutionaries. After signing the docu-ment, Bishop Tang acknowledged that although the Communist Party was comprised of atheists and materialists who wanted to destroy reli-gion, at this point they were allowing religion to exist. He promised to administer his diocese well. The head of the Bureau of Religious Affairs made it clear that he was no longer bishop of Canton.

Taken to live with priests, including one who served as bishop, Bishop Tang felt peaceful and yet isolated and deserted. A woman claiming to be Catholic was assigned to watch over him. Bishop Tang doubted that she was actually Catholic as he never once saw her kneel during the con-secration or receive Holy Communion. When Catholics or foreigners came to the residence to see him, she told them that he was away visit-ing the doctor. Occasionally, visitors saw him on the terrace; they knelt and asked for his blessing. A French priest brought him books, but his guardian took them. It was a struggle for Bishop Tang to get permission to go to confession, much less say Mass. Eventually, in September, he was allowed to begin saying Mass at a side altar, and Catholics soon started coming to his Masses.

In a Canton hospital, Bishop Tang was diagnosed as having cancer of the colon. He announced that he wanted to go to Hong Kong for treatment, adding that the government would find it difficult to take responsibility for leaving him to suffer and die in Canton. At an October meeting of the Bureau of Religious Affairs, two questions were raised. The first was whether or not the diocese of Canton needed a bishop, and the second was whether or not Dominic Tang Yee-ming was worthy of the office. The members of the meeting agreed unanimously, with government approval, that he should be bishop of Canton. The Canton Catholics and the Vatican were aware of his plans to celebrate Mass publicly and to preach. Bishop Tang threw himself into pastoral work in the fall of 1980.

In November 1980, he was granted permission to go to Hong Kong for medical treatment. When an official of the Bureau of Religious Affairs asked him if he would go to see the pope, Bishop Tang replied that he would if he were invited. He stated that the Catholic Church was closely connected with the Vatican and wanted to know if he would be allowed to establish relations. There was no direct answer. His permit for Hong Kong covered a one-year visit, after which he was to return to Canton. Given presents for his family in Hong Kong, he went to the Canton police station to cancel his ration card, although he kept his residency permit. On the eve of his departure, Bishop Tang told officers of the City Bureau of Religious Affairs quite frankly that they had gone too far in carrying out policies. Later, at a farewell tea party, Bishop Tang said that the state of his illness would determine when he would return.

Surgery in Hong Kong proved successful, and on Christmas morning 1980, Bishop Tang said Mass at the cathedral. He celebrated his fiftieth anniversary as a Jesuit in Hong Kong. He was shown a book in which his name had been placed on the list of the dead in 1969, and he also saw the papal bull of his appointment as a bishop in 1951 for the first time; it had not been possible to send the bull to Canton at the time. There was discussion about the possibility of his meeting with the pope in the Philippines or Japan in 1981. Bishop Tang was asked by Secretary of State Agostino Cardinal Casaroli to contact the Chinese government in Peking and build a bridge. Then he was asked to meet the pope in Rome.

In April of 1981, Bishop Tang flew to Rome, accompanied by Father Franco Belfiori, S.J. Immediately upon his arrival in Rome, he was summoned by the pope. Other meetings and sightseeing followed, and Bishop Tang celebrated Mass at the Basilica of St. Cecilia; he also celebrated Mass on Vatican radio, praying for the Church in China. During his visit to the Chinese embassy, he was told that in order for China to establish relations with the Vatican, the Vatican would have to break off relations with Taiwan. Actually, during the Cultural Revolution, the pope had made a gesture to the People's Republic of China by recalling the nuncio from Taiwan and leaving only a chargé d'affaires, something that both the Taiwanese government and the local church resented. Peking's response was to continue its attacks on the church.

Invited back to Rome after visits to other European and American cities, Bishop Tang found himself appointed archbishop of Canton. The pope was still recovering from the injuries of an assassination attempt, so Basil Cardinal Hume of Westminster presided over the Solemn Concelebrated Mass in St. Peter's. The Holy Father appeared at the window overlooking St. Peter's Square to bless the people. A recorded message of the pope was broadcast, and more than three hundred cardinals and bishops concelebrated. Archbishop Matthew Kia of Taiwan was one of the participants in the ceremony.

Chinese priests and sisters residing in Rome were delighted. Newspapers wrote of a bridge being built between the Vatican and China. However, one week after the celebration, Peking attacked the Vatican for interfering in the internal affairs of China. Bishop Tang was identified as a traitor, and the Chinese Catholic Patriotic Association of Canton announced that he was dismissed from his position as bishop of

*Canton. Later statements from Bishop Tang regarding his allegiance to
the pope further angered Peking.*

Archbishop Tang died in the United States in 1995.

❖   ❖   ❖

ON DECEMBER 8, 1981, filled with the spirit of the Immaculate Conception, I wrote my farewell letter. It was important for me to get word to Father Frank, asking him to thank my brothers and fathers in Christ for their prayers, which strengthened me. On the tenth, Eddie and I boarded the bus for the long trip to Anhui province. We spent the night at the station hostel, and the next morning, before leaving, I penned another letter to Father Frank to which, once we arrived at our destination, I added on another slip only these simple facts: "Dec. 11, at 11 A.M. back on the farm. Good-bye . . . and prayers." Eddie took the letter and the note back to Shanghai and sent them via Hong Kong to Los Gatos, where they arrived as a Christmas gift. The following January, I celebrated a double feast: my solar birthday on the eleventh and my lunar birthday on the twelfth, letting Father Frank know in yet another letter of my prayers and greetings for Ours and the extended family of brothers and sisters, aunts and uncles, cousins, nieces and nephews.

At White Lake Farm, I was considered retired. Actually, I was hoping to procure a teaching job at nearby Anhui University, but despite glowing letters of recommendation, that did not materialize. You might think that I had a lot of free time, but I noticed that some days wasted away in idle chitchat. Still, I profited from the sunshine to practice shadowboxing in order to stay physically fit. I also read by day; evenings were not conducive to reading or writing because light attracted mosquitoes. I managed to devour many books, magazines, and news articles. A great consolation came when books not available to me directly eventually found their way to me, having been handed off and mailed from one person to another.

Although it took a long time to arrive, shipped literally on a slow boat to China, Father Frank sent me a copy of Father George Dunne's *Generation of Giants,* a truly scholarly work published twenty years previously, in 1962, on the early Jesuit missionaries in China. The volume was dedicated to the sweet memory of our mentors, Yves Henry and Auguste Haouisée, giants in their own right. Reading a book of this stature, when it is to one's taste and delectation, underscores the transcendence of time and space. Whether on a desert island, in a subway, or in a prison camp, one feels the centuries dissolved, oceans dried up, distance annihilated, and reader and author become one.

My raving about the book doesn't mean that I was uncritical. In the foreword, George stated frankly that he had very few debts, but that those he had were substantial. He wrote, "My heaviest debt is to Francis A. Rouleau, S.J., who saved me from many errors of omission and commission and out of the immense reservoir of his own knowledge generously filled the many lacunae in my own." In a letter to Father Frank written on September 8, 1982, on Our Lady's birthday, I congratulated him for his incalculable contribution to the opus. At the same time, I pointed out that the author, in acknowledging his heaviest debt to Father Frank, had passed the buck for the minor inaccuracies left unnoticed. For example, Paoting was not south of Peking but north, the people of Macao were Macaonese and not Macaoist (*ist* connotates a follower, as in Maoist), and Li Ma-t'ou should have been written without the aspirate. I indicated that in modern Pinyin, the name was Li Madou.

I wondered why there was no mention of Ricci's literary name, *Hsi T'ai,* which appeared in all the other books. I was also critical of the black-and-white rendering of the posthumous portrait of Ricci by Brother Manoel Yu as it appeared in *Generation of Giants.* The original, having been brought to Rome in 1614 by Nicholas Trigault, S.J., was hung in 1617 in the Jesuit residence of the Gesù and remains there alongside the portraits of St. Ignatius and St. Francis Xavier. I had seen a picture card of the original and remembered that the emblem of the Society of Jesus was in dark crimson with the letters *IHS* scarcely visible but still noticeable. On the other hand, in the black-and-white version in the book, the centerpiece of the emblem is blurred even though the rays are noticeable. To my thinking, one could mistake the blur in the *Generation of Giants* illustration as a cover-up.

But mostly I was in awe of George's work, joining him in musing over the great ifs of history. Not only did George raise the question that asked how Christianity might have evolved in China if the church had not condemned the Chinese Rites, but he also gave us the opportunity to ponder obedience. The Jesuit missionaries, complacent and confident that the 1656 decree from Rome permitting the practice of the Rites under the conditions observed by the Jesuits was the final word, were too busy with their work to respond to repeated appeals from the general for documentation to assist theologians in the defense of their cause. Apparently, they were unaware of how controversial the issue of the Rites was in Europe, and so they responded too late. One has to ask what might have happened if, instead of ignoring the appeals, they had obediently responded with promptness and diligence.

So many books found their way to the house in Shanghai that Willie would copy down the titles and send the list to me at White Lake Farm, asking me to make a selection, which he would then forward. I had hit the literary jackpot—Charles Dickens and Robert Louis Stevenson, John Henry Newman and Bishop Fulton Sheen, Joyce Kilmer's *Anthology* and G. K. Chesterton's *The Everlasting Man.* I read Thomas Merton's autobiography, *The Seven Storey Mountain,* and also Bing Crosby's autobiography, *Call Me Lucky.* In early July of 1982, I was blessed with a copy of the *Contemporary Reading of the Spiritual Exercises of St. Ignatius* by David Fleming, S.J.

The *Contemporary Reading* became my spiritual reading in preparation for the feast day of St. Ignatius of Loyola on July 31, a day that

I would share with my Jesuit confrères all over the world. Additionally, a friend of Father Frank's made sure that I received copies of *Reader's Digest* and *National Geographic*. Even the ads were of interest to me. The Hong Kong English editions of magazines had fewer ads than the U.S. editions, and the Chinese editions still fewer. Conscious that the press, including ads, could be used to manipulate public opinion, I nevertheless found the ads refreshing in their approach to sales persuasion, in their artistic presentation, and in their upbeat mood. As for the joy of living, I made the connection between *Reader's Digest* and its headquarters: Pleasantville, New York.

During this period, I was introduced to the notion of gender-inclusive language and to many new words. Once Father Frank used the word *bash* in a letter to me; fortunately, a recent copy of the Random House paperback dictionary provided an explanation: "a wildly good time." And the word *mod* was defined in an issue of *Contemporary English Studies* as "extremely up-to-date and fashionable as in the style of clothes, make-up, or art."

Actually, the word was familiar to me, but I looked it up anyway, as a magazine article had described mod liturgies enhanced by music pulsating like a rock beat as priests, trying fervently to be relevant, brought religious services into the coffeehouse, the factory, and the supermarket. All this reading material kept my mind busy; the magazines were intellectual hay for me. In a letter to Father Frank, I asked him if he knew that in modern times, newspapers had become fodder for cows. I was reminded of what Chesterton had said of Thomas Aquinas (also on my reading list): the bellow of the dumb ox could be heard all over the world.

While I was at White Lake Farm, my nephew Eddie was trying to get to the United States. Through the intervention of U.S. Congressman Father Robert Drinan, S.J., whom Father Frank had contacted, Eddie was granted a visa. He made it to California, where he was welcomed by Father Frank and his family. The reference to this meeting was the reason I had to look up the word *bash* in the dictionary. In his letter, Father Frank also described the occasion as a hilarious time, and in subsequent correspondence he would refer to Eddie as the apple of his eye. As for Father Drinan, one day he would receive a gift from me: the old shaving mug that had served as a chalice during my clandestine Masses in Shanghai.

The relationship with Father Frank, taking on various forms—father-son, Jonathan-David, Simeon–Little Jesus, *pater in Filio, filius in Filio, filius Mariae in Filio*—was reflected in the way I addressed him in my letters. Over forty-five years had gone by since our first meeting on July 27, 1937, when I had set out to meet another priest, providentially encountering Father Frank instead. It was from White Lake Farm in the summer of 1982 that I wrote to him about the humility I felt in telling him on board the *Asama Maru*, as I was leaving for the Novitiate, to love Jesus with all his heart. What I should have stated instead were my intentions to follow the gleam, and I should have expressed my gratitude for his magnanimous devotion.

In the words of Ronald Knox, the English monsignor whose translation of the Bible I never ceased to admire, I told Father Frank that "no nursing mother would have done more for her child." I admitted not only feeling tongue-tied in my youthful days but also mind blank. I assured him that each time he held Eddie in affectionate embrace that I was responding as well with the same Peter-and-Paul sign of love. Holding all of Ours in my heart, I held Father Frank in the very center with the Heart of hearts. This was the letter, penned on the Feast of St. Ignatius as I joined Father Frank in the Ignatian prayer we call the Suscipe, that caused him to cry like a baby while he sat reading in Los Gatos.

Though Father Frank had many spiritual children and often spoke of them, he managed to write long letters to me frequently. He referred to the letters as marathon missives, and indeed each was rich and edifying, with descriptions and colloquies and gentle exhortations. He claimed that my letters, usually consisting of four half-pages on onionskin paper, were brief, and he referred to them as mere slips. Just as he did in 1948 when I was in Yangchow, Father Frank urged me to write more. It turns out that he particularly liked my Yangchow letters with the accounts of Father Farmer and Jeeps. And so our correspondence continued, and our mutual connections grew.

George Wong, S.J., as an ex-convict farmworker, 1976.

Family gathering in Shanghai, Christmas 1985. Nephew Johnny and his wife, June; their daughter Mary; George Wong, S.J.; K.K. ("little Iggie"); cousin Pearl; Rosie at age 80; brother Willie and wife, Julie; oldest nephew, Iggie (Ignatius). K.K.'s mother is working the evening shift.

Father Edward Malatesta visits the Wong family in Shanghai, 1988.

Father Wong as an English teacher in Shanghai, 1979.

George Wong, S.J., visits the grave of Francis Rouleau, S.J., in Santa Clara, 1992.

✥ 19 ✥

The Fourth Vow

*A*T THE TIME *of the Communist takeover in 1949 there were three million Catholics in China. A widely held view was that most of the Catholics were simply rice Christians and therefore the religion would die when the churches were closed down and when foreign funding was cut off. Although in some places there is no news of Catholic or Christian practices, in other areas whole families continued over the years to gather for prayer. Post–Cultural Revolution visitors to China were surprised to find religion thriving in villages where the walls of peasant homes displayed portraits of Jesus and Mary next to pictures of Mao and Marx.*

Priests in prison and labor camps made converts who, after their release, took their new faith with them to their home villages. Prayers and meditations especially suited to the oppressed were cherished and copied and spread to many regions. Christians baptized Christians. Little girls of past generations, abandoned in infancy by their parents and raised in orphanages by the sisters, grew up to marry and then nurture the Catholic faith in their own households. This, in spite of the continued renewal of anti-Catholic campaigns, as in 1973 when Mao distributed one million pamphlets about the "murder" of orphans at Zikawei twenty years before.

Still, parents feared even teaching their children prayers during the Cultural Revolution; children were encouraged to report any household religious activity. Following Mao's death in 1976, some priests returned to their dioceses thinking that they would be able to engage in their ministry. Occasionally, party leaders in rural areas closed their eyes to the religious activities practiced publicly. However, while not able to penetrate the countryside, the Catholic Patriotic Association reemerged and began overseeing the churches, especially in the cities.

In the 1980s, foreigners were joined by Archbishop Dominic Tang in speaking of an underground church. Eventually, members of the Catholic Patriotic Association, in complaining about the Vatican's authorizing the ordination of underground bishops, acknowledged the existence of an underground movement that they had previously denied. Some elderly priests, released after twenty or thirty years in prisons and labor camps, preferred, like Father Wong, to return to prison or to labor camps rather than be disloyal to the Holy See. Not allowed to carry out their ministry publicly, they were and are revered by the faithful, who treat their houses as shrines and who form long lines for confession if allowed.

Appeals to Rome for additional priests resulted in bishops being given the ability to name and ordain their successors as well as to appoint bishops to neighboring dioceses when there was no bishop. Although the intent was to make sure that the people were not left without shepherds, the results have sometimes been unfortunate. In some areas, more than one bishop has been appointed for the same diocese. Often the secret bishops have had little pastoral experience, and young priests are ordained with inadequate formation. Moreover, some underground Catholics engage in superstitious practices, thus unintentionally offering the Communists the opportunity to equate religion with superstition.

Clandestine religious activity is severely punished by the Communist authorities. Priests of the public church receive a salary, whereas underground priests, released from prison, may be permitted jobs like sweeping streets. However, if caught in religious activity, they may find themselves in jail again or, at least, removed from access to the public. There are stories of informers, sometimes Catholics who renounced their faith in the early days of Communism and then returned to those they had betrayed to seek forgiveness. Having regained the trust of underground priests, they were able to inform the police of where the clergy kept their correspondence from abroad and of whom the priests had helped with foreign money and medicine. A priest and a party member whom he baptized in the presence of her sponsor, a renegade Catholic who had supposedly come back to the church, were arrested the following day. Catholic visitors to China face a special dilemma. They are expected to attend the public festivities put on by the Patriotic Church. However, their visits to underground Catholics put the latter at risk of being arrested for having contact with foreigners.

The number of Catholics in China today is given officially as about three million—the same as in 1949. The unofficial number is about ten million, the majority of whom practice their faith openly and who see no contradiction between attending services in the churches administered by the Patriotic Association and remaining in union with the one universal church. While there are two camps, one known as the public church and the other as the underground church, and bitter, even violent, clashes do exist between them, there is no organized subversive movement amounting to a schism in the church. Nevertheless, there is a striking difference between the underground church and the public church: the former has many martyrs while the latter has none.

❖   ❖   ❖

A CHINESE LADY who had helped me with the bulletin board at Christ the King Church when I was assistant pastor between 1953 and 1955 had recently lost her British husband. Emigrating to New York in 1982, Betty Crighton Lee traveled to California within three months, and Father James Chevedden, S.J., met her at Eddie's house, where she was staying, and took her to visit Father Frank in Los Gatos. She gave him firsthand news of me. She had lost contact with me after my arrest, but we got together again in the 1970s during my home leaves from White Lake Farm when the Cultural Revolution was still de rigueur. Even though she had very little money at the time, she procured the cloth to make me padded jackets to take back to the farm. And it was through the help of her husband that I was offered the teaching job at the Foreign Language Institute. I baptized her daughter Carole, and though I had not been available to baptize her son, he was named David at my suggestion. Eventually there would be a little granddaughter to whom I gave the name of Regina.

When Betty met Father Frank face to face in Los Gatos, she addressed him as her dear spiritual grandpa. Thanks to Betty and her connections, my correspondence with Father Frank continued, and sometimes she wrote to him as well. Through Betty, Father Frank would know that I spent from August to November of 1982 in Shanghai. Having gone there for dental work, I was retained for questioning by the police regarding Jesuits arrested in 1981. She reported other things too. For example, she told him that after thirty years of silence about religion in China, she was finally able to enroll in a course at her parish in New York. There, learning how much the church had changed, she found it surprising that the same church that had excommunicated Martin Luther now recognized that he had been right.

In 1983 White Lake Farm experienced another flood, and—I took the date as a sign—on July 31, the Feast of St. Ignatius of Loyola, I was allowed to return to Shanghai. Due to my age, which was now sixty-five, I was also allowed to transfer, albeit temporarily, my residence there but without the benefit of rice, meat, or cloth coupons. Matters may have been different if I had responded favorably to the renewed request of the Patriotic Association, but I continued to refuse. As always, the California Jesuits helped me out materially as well as spiritually. I was able to resume teaching at the Foreign Language Institute operated by the government and at the same time, in the spirit of ecumenism, taught English at the seminary operated by the government. Moreover, I became secretary to the rector, Bishop Aloysius Jin Luxian.

In a sense I was leading a double life, and in a sense I wasn't. My not being part of the public church was obvious even if I taught at their seminary and worked for their rector; my underground associations were not. Visitors came from abroad, and if they came to my house, I would observe a government car posted in the street for surveillance. When word came that Jerry Brown was visiting Shanghai and wanted to meet me, I went to his hotel in the evening but insisted that we go for a walk. Circling the hotel on foot, we probably were together for less than half an hour, during which I answered his questions about the public church and the underground church in a very limited fashion.

As for my work in the seminary and with the rector, I was once asked to serve as interpreter for the acting rector of Our Lady of Help of Christians Church when some foreigners came to visit. When lunchtime rolled around, I was ready to withdraw, but the acting rector insisted that I join the group for the meal. However, the Patriotic Association official made his disapproval of the luncheon invitation clear. So the acting rector ended up withdrawing from the guests, following me instead to the fathers' dining room. Aware that he was generously manifesting his solidarity with me, I was nevertheless uneasy about the embarrassing circumstances. I don't know if this incident was related or not to the fact that one day in 1987 I would be told that my services were no longer needed at the seminary.

A letter from Father Frank announced the 1981 death in Los Angeles of Sister Candida, Gladys Wei. In attempting to renew contact with her a few years before, he learned that she was suffering from Lou Gehrig's disease. After my arrest in 1955, Gladys managed to get to Hong Kong and from there to Taiwan; eventually she returned to the motherhouse of the Sisters of Social Service, where her final years were spent in increasingly deteriorating health. My Ignatian formation included cultivating indifference to the point of not preferring health over sickness, but that was for myself. It remains a mystery to me today as to why Our Lord took her—she was truly serving God as she served others—instead of me. I was grieved by the news of her death and would have gladly changed places with her.

In 1984, a letter arrived in the handwriting of Sister Mary Celeste, whom I had first known as Joan, the young niece of Father Frank. Before opening it, I understood the terrible pain its news would bring me. Father Frank died on February 21, 1984, and no amount of understanding that it was his time to go and that he was prepared and ready to surrender his spirit could alleviate the immediate and deep pain I felt. When Gladys sent me that letter in our youthful days announcing the rupture of our friendship, I could not eat or sleep. Throughout the years I never again experienced such anguish until Sister Celeste's letter. Not able to eat or sleep, I wept bitter, confused tears. Devastated about my loss, I also rejoiced at having shared forty-six years with him, though only a few of them placed us in proximity. The words of William Wordsworth came to mind as he wrote that "few could know when Lucy ceased to be. But she is in her grave, and, oh, the difference to me!" My heart felt that he was in his grave—and, oh, the difference to me! Thank God for the Communion of Saints!

Recall that I had only pronounced the simple vows of the Society of Jesus, and these during the novitiate. As I had not performed sufficiently at my theology oral examination in Latin, I was not eligible to pronounce solemn vows. Simple vows are those of poverty, chastity, and obedience with special emphasis on poverty as well as a promise not to aspire to the office of bishop. Solemn vows are the first three plus the fourth vow of obedience to the pope. There are various ways of expressing the tenor of these vows. For practical purposes, the difference is that those who have pronounced solemn vows, having attained a higher level, may find themselves called to serve as superiors and consultors. This hierarchical arrangement seemed suitable enough, for I recognized that we all have different talents and different roles. Over time the Society of Jesus made some changes, de-emphasizing the role of the performance at the theology examination as a coefficient in the formula to determine the eligibility of the pronouncement of the fourth vow.

In my case, God knows of my willingness to serve the pope in the vineyard of the Lord, though I fostered no ambitions with regard to leadership or direction in the Society. My apostolate was character-ized more by surrendering to God's will than by leading the charge. Some foreign Jesuits staying at a Shanghai hotel were aware that word had come from the superior general that I was to pronounce my solemn vows. During my visit with them at the hotel, they urged me to overlook the lack of candles and form, and simply kneel right there in the room and make this solemn profession.

It wasn't the absence of candles, incense, or flowers that caused me to hesitate. I explained to them frankly that doing so would be risky, for at any minute the door could be swung open by someone posing as an employee of the hotel on the pretext of making sure that everyone was comfortable; in reality, a check would be made of who was present and what was happening. No sooner had I declared the intrusion as a real possibly than a quick knock on the door was followed by its opening abruptly. An inquiry about our comfort was made as the employee's eyes scanned the room to determine who was present.

In the first part of 1991 a letter from the Jesuit superior in Hong Kong, Italian Father Franco Belfiori, announced that I should seek the vow formula from a confrère in Shanghai. But this letter didn't satisfy the aged confrère whom I contacted; he wanted to see not a letter but an official document from Rome. Hearing of this, Father Belfiori wrote again that I was to go ahead with my vows, and this time the Shanghai confrère was satisfied. Actually the delay was a blessing, since I attach a special significance to dates. In 1991, on April 22, which happens to be the Feast of Mary, Mother of the Society of Jesus, with a devoted and grateful heart in the presence of Christ and all the saints, I pronounced during the celebration of the Eucharist my solemn vows, professing my willingness to be loyal to the successor of Peter.

This was done at the residence of Father Gabriel Chen, in his presence and that of his sister, who was a nun who took care of him in his poor health. Also present was a second nun who shared the residence with them. And, yes, there were candles lit on that occasion—and lit again when, under the authorization of the Jesuit superior communicating through special channels, I received the solemn vows of Father Shen Tseng Li, the diocesan priest who was now a Jesuit and who had been with me in the prison cell following our sentencing in 1962. The candles were lit a third time in my home in Shanghai—we let the convenience of the location override our concern about surveillance—as Father Francis Wang pronounced his solemn vows. He now lives with me in Los Gatos.

✣ 20 ✣

Los Gatos

*J*UST AS MAJOR *changes in the Roman Catholic Church came about following Vatican II, the Society of Jesus evolved. When Father Wong returned to Los Gatos, he did not find young men picking grapes in the vineyard or roaming the halls in cassocks. Instead the novices—less numerous and a bit older these days—were living in communities closer to the world they would serve. Working in the vineyard of the Lord had taken on a broader meaning. Though they were all scholars, some, working among the poor and motivated not by politics but by the promise of the Good News of Jesus Christ, would find their apostolates in social justice. They might be closer to the world, and yet customs suitable for seculars would not be introduced into community life. Neither would those deemed appropriate for monastic life.*

A Jesuit emerging from years of isolation might be dismayed that his confrères appear less devoted to the Sacred Heart, for example. But what could be interpreted as a decrease in devotion to the Sacred Heart has been recognized by the Society of Jesus as the general declining appeal of outmoded devotional practices. Acknowledging that devotion to the Sacred Heart is an excellent and tested form of dedication to Christ Jesus, the Society urges theologians to search out ways of presenting this devotion that are better suited to various regions and persons. Such is what St. Ignatius had in mind when he built into the Constitutions of the Society of Jesus room to adapt to a changing world in order to work for the greater glory of God.

Changes exist in things like the ages of those entering the Society of Jesus, the role of psychology in evaluating their maturity and readiness to serve, the emphasis placed on respect and appreciation for cultural diversity, the place and course of study, and the norms for the promotion of priests to the profession of four vows. On the other hand, the integration of prayer and the active life has remained constant. The Society of Jesus is a dynamic branch of an organic church.

❖   ❖   ❖

A FERVENT WISH of mine had been to be reunited with Father Frank sometime before the Eternal Banquet, but that was not the will of God. Day after day and year after year, I felt in touch with my Jesuit brothers in Christ and with the universal church and always felt the presence of God, Our Lady, and the saints. This all sounds very spiritual, and so it should, but the fact is that the material played a role as well. Just as the Eucharist enables us to touch and taste the real presence of Christ, who is the bread of life, the tangible care of the California Jesuits, manifested in the food and vitamins they enabled my family to send to me, helped me remain physically strong and spiritually connected to them. I was conscious of having no problem, in general terms, of transcending time and space but do admit to a specific difficulty. It was hardest with regard to Father

Francis. I longed to see him again and to crawl into his arms just as the little Jesus was held by Simeon. And yet, I was also aware, vaguely, for I didn't dwell on this type of meditation, that Simeon had gone to a peaceful death with the knowledge that Jesus would grow up even though his adulthood would be marked by pain and suffering. Things may not have happened in the same sequence, but I can't help feeling that Father Francis had gone to his death in peace knowing that I had grown up. I felt that he was present at the Eucharist on the occasion of my solemn profession of the fourth vow. That sacrament sealed the commitment we had made to each other like Jonathan and David before the Lord.

The Italian premier Giulio Andreotti visited Li Peng, premier of China, regarding Italy's gift of more Fiat ambulances to the People's Republic of China. The first ambulances had played a significant role in the Tiananmen Square incident of 1989, running down student demonstrators and then hauling their bodies away. Having stopped in Hong Kong, where he met up with Jesuit Father Franco Belfiori, Andreotti was made aware of my particular situation and intervened on my behalf with Li Peng when he got to Peking. Very soon after Andreotti's 1991 visit to the premier, I was summoned to the police station, where I was told that my passport application would be approved. Both my sisters and my brother, Willie, had gone to their eternal rest; from my generation only my sister-in-law, Julie, remained, and she was in California visiting Eddie.

Knowing that I would be leaving China, Betty Crighton Lee made a special trip from New York to Shanghai so that she could accompany me to California. In December 1991, having said farewell to my nephews and their spouses and offspring in Shanghai, I arrived with Betty at San Francisco Airport to be greeted by Eddie and his mother, Julie. They took me to Los Gatos, the old Novitiate that now houses elder Jesuits as well as the offices of the California Province. I was received by Father Provincial Paul Belcher, whom I had escorted once when he visited China to the Shrine of Our Lady of Sheshan, known in the Shanghai dialect as Zosé.

Many changes had occurred at Los Gatos. Even though I was in what was still called the Novitiate, it no longer served as a novitiate; it had become the Sacred Heart Jesuit Center, and I would live there with my elder confrères. Our routine is not as structured or as formal as in our novitiate days, but I think that the superiors—first Father Gregory Aherne, then Father Leo Hombach, and now Father Richard Cobb—do a good job of helping build community life. We are invited to concelebrate our community Mass, which is held on Sundays. Birthdays are posted, and once a month we hold birthday celebrations.

Feast days are observed, marked by a special menu. But meals are served cafeteria style. Nowadays it doesn't matter where you sit. You simply find a table with an empty chair; it may be the same table each time, and you may find the same companions day in and day out. There are no rules about silence or using Latin or listening to edifying reading. Not interested in joining in conversations about sports, I usually end up at a table that Leo refers to as "the think tank," since the men like to linger in discussion. There is no challenge to avoid superfluous conversation. One of my reasons for drifting toward the think tank is that, with no teeth of my own, I take a long time to eat. Since I can count on my companions to debate and discuss issues at length, I know that I can finish my meal.

My arrival in Los Gatos was followed by medical visits and procedures—effective surgery on the rectum that had suffered from eating rice husks and treatment for the sores left from the attacks of rice-paddy leeches on my legs. With prayer groups to lead, Masses to be said for a neighboring community of sisters and for the children of the Chinese community who gather at St. Clare's Church, and friendships to maintain, my life has been full but not necessarily routine. I keep up a correspondence with many spiritual children, meeting with them and their offspring whenever possible. Twice I have traveled to New York, staying with Betty and her grandchildren. On both occasions in New York I baptized grandchildren of William

James, whom I first knew in Shanghai when he, having just gradu-ated from St. Francis Xavier College, entered Aurora University. Later he would become a doctor attached to a hospital in New York and, with his wife, raise four children. I would visit friends in Arizona and give talks to schoolchildren there.

I reviewed the excellent anthology to be used in courses on spiri-tuality in education compiled by Mary Louise Baly Meissner, whom I first met when she was doing work in Shanghai. Often I am the guest in the San Francisco home of Mary and John Liu, the parents of one of my private pupils from Shanghai. I even went to Mexico in 1996 and, walking along the beach and enjoying the sunsets of Puerto Vallarta, was reminded of the reference to the "flaming monstrance of the West" in a poem by Francis Thompson entitled "Orient Ode." But the highlight of my life as a priest occurred within months of my arrival at the Sacred Heart Jesuit Center in Los Gatos. Father Provincial Paul Belcher asked me if I felt up to making a trip to Rome.

✤ 21 ✤

Pilgrimage to Rome

*F*ATHER WONG TRAVELED *to Rome in 1992 for the canonization of Claude La Colombière (1641–1682), the French Jesuit spiritual director of St. Margaret Mary who encouraged La Colombière in teaching devotion to the Sacred Heart. In England during a time of persecution against Catholics, he served as chaplain to the Duchess of York. The Test Act of 1673 required all those aspiring to public office to declare that they did not believe in the real presence of Our Lord in the Eucharist. Claude La Colombière, who took great consolation in the Eucharist, was falsely accused of speaking against the king and spent three weeks in a dungeon before being exiled from England. The only thing he could be charged with was converting people to Catholicism.*

During his visit to Rome in 1992, Father Wong called on Guilio Andreotti; their meeting took place just as Andreotti's political life began to unravel. A Christian Democrat politician and life senator who was

seven times prime minister, Andreotti would be going on trial for selling
favors to the Mafia in exchange for political support and, along with four
others, would be charged with the 1979 murder of a journalist investi-
gating Mafia ties. After the first trial started but before the second began,
Andreotti was photographed with Pope John Paul II as the Holy Father
took his hands between his own. The Christian Democrats, in power
from 1945 until 1992, had the support of the United States as well as the
Vatican, both intent on combating Communism. Many Italians today
think highly of the former prime minister whose age—he was born in
1919, one year after Father Wong—makes it unlikely that he will live to
see the end of his trials. Others in Italy, no longer finding it necessary to
support coalition governments against the Italian Communist Party, are
disgusted by all those who engaged in corrupt politics.

In this complex world we see a former Italian prime minister, cred-
ited with weakening the Communist Party in his own country, obtain
from the premier of the People's Republic of China the freedom of a
Jesuit priest. A man often seen in prayer in the churches of Italy,
Andreotti, like Claude La Colombière, takes great consolation in the
Eucharist. Deemed a hero by many loyal followers, known as Uncle to
some members of the Mafia, and called a murderer by his accusers,
Andreotti is for Father Wong an angel.

❖   ❖   ❖

THE OCCASION OF the trip to Rome was the canonization of
Blessed Claude La Colombière on May 31, 1992, which was also
the forty-first anniversary of my ordination. What a thrill it was to
visit the heart of Catholicism and visit the historic monuments like
the half-tottering Colosseum where the early Roman Christians won
the palm of martyrdom! I was also in awe of the divine grandeur and
magnificence of Renaissance art, sculpture, and architecture as
embodied in the stupendously majestic Basilica of St. Peter or as

exemplified in the strikingly graphic frescoes of Michelangelo in the recently renovated Sistine Chapel. As for the richness of baroque splendor in the Jesuit Church of Gesù, let me pass it by in silent admiration and appreciation and continue by leading you on a walk through the dimly lit catacombs, pausing there to pray for the underground church in China and elsewhere.

Indeed I was privileged to say Mass at the tomb of St. Peter, the prince of the apostles and our first pope, and likewise I was graced to offer the Sacred Liturgy in the bedroom of St. Ignatius Loyola where he rendered his soul to the Divine Master on July 31, 1556. While in Rome, accompanied by Father Joseph Pittau, whom I had met previously in Shanghai when he accepted the solemn vows of my confrère Father Francis Xavier Wang, I also took the opportunity to call upon Premier Giulio Andreotti to thank him for his intervention on my behalf with the Chinese premier. I told him how at the beginning of my imprisonment I had thought of the angel who led St. Peter out of prison. Thirty-six years after my arrival at the Railway Station Jail in Shanghai, Andreotti acted as my angel, gaining my liberation. During this meeting, he asked what else he could do for the church in China, and I replied that his continued prayerful support of religious freedom in my homeland would be deeply appreciated. This was indeed a memorable moment.

Most notable of all, however—I count it as a sheer blessing and a grace unique in my eighty years—was the concelebration of the canonization Mass with our Holy Father Pope John Paul II. Among the ten concelebrants were two non-Jesuits, Monsignor Séguy, the bishop of Autun diocese in which Paray-le-Monial is located (and where St. Claude spent several years as spiritual father to the Visitation nun St. Margaret Mary Alacoque) and the superior general of the Eudists, Father Drouin. (The Eudists are also great devotees of the Sacred Heart.) Besides myself, the eight concelebrating Jesuits included Father Superior Peter-Hans Kolvenbach; his assistant for France, Jacques Gellard, who was also the provincial of France, father superior of the residence of Paray-le-Monial; the secretary general of the Apostleship of Prayer, Father John Vessels; two Jesuit bishops, one from Lima, Peru, and the other from Ahmedabad, India; and Paolo Molinari, who was in charge of the canonization case.

The climax came when the Holy Father pronounced in Latin the solemn formula of canonization: "In honor of the Holy and Undivided Trinity . . . by the Authority of Our Lord Jesus Christ . . . and of Ours . . . we discreetly judge and we definitively proclaim that Blessed Claude La Colombière is a saint." There was a resounding "Amen" from the whole sanctuary and basilica, and a prolonged ovation.

Throughout the awe-inspiring two-hour ceremony what was going on in my heart of hearts? It was a consciousness that I was not there alone with those in Rome, but there we were in union with the whole universal church throughout the world from the rising of the sun to its setting on that eventful day in May. And in particular I was united in heart and soul with my confrères in the Society of Jesus—those from the California Province and those in China and everywhere. I was mindful as well, *specialissimo modo,* of the faithful Catholics, on the Mainland and in Taiwan, Hong Kong, and Macao—in a word, in China. This grace-inspired thought made me supremely happy. Conscious of this as a living expression of God's love, I did not wish for anything more.

At the end of this jubilant ceremony all the ten concelebrants filed out with the Holy Father to the place in front of the shrine of the pietà, and there, in one straight line, we had our group photograph taken. Afterward His Holiness shook hands with each one of us in appreciation for our liturgical concelebration with him. When at last he came to me, I bowed in reverence and esteem to kiss the sacred ring of Our Lord's Fisherman.

I must pause here to pay tribute to the magnanimity of Father Frank Parrish, S.J., the octogenarian director of the Apostleship of Prayer in the Los Angeles diocese and of the Sacred Heart Program, for it was he who so generously gave up his place to let me concelebrate at the papal altar. This same Father Parrish had in the spring of 1991 initiated the prayers of intercession to Blessed Claude La Colombière for the miraculous cure of the former Jesuit missionary prisoner in China Father John Houle, who suffered from pulmonary fibrosis. That miracle made for the canonization of our new Jesuit saint. Both Fathers Houle and Parrish were humbly content to be in the pew just outside the sanctuary in St. Peter's.

The day after the canonization Mass there was a papal audience given to the worldwide delegates and members of the Apostleship of Prayer (about one thousand of them), headed up by Father John Vessels, S.J., in the Hall of Pope Paul VI in the Vatican. Again I was privileged to have a seat on the stage next to Father General Peter-Hans Kolvenbach and the present rector of the prestigious Gregorian University in Rome, Father Joseph Pittau. I really felt very small except that the thought of my solidarity with my Jesuit confrères buoyed me up and made me happy. During that audience Father Pittau introduced me to the Holy Father in Italian. "Parla italiano?" the pope asked.

"No," I replied for Father Pittau, "I speak English." And I continued excitedly, "Thank you, Holy Father, for all your prayers for China."

He reassured me, in English, "I pray for China every day." What a consolation to hear these words of encouragement from our Holy Father John Paul II! At the end of the papal audience, as he was passing by me, waving his hand, he looked at me and said just this one word, "China!" This was his way of greeting not me alone but all of China. Indeed our Holy Father has more than once publicly expressed his keen and earnest desire to visit China and even to make a pilgrimage to the semibasilica of Our Lady of Help of Christians on Sheshan (Zosé) Hill, some twenty miles southwest of Shanghai. Just as my dream of meeting the pope personally has come true, so may the Good Lord grant Pope John Paul II the favor of visiting China before long. Amen! Amen!

✢ 22 ✢

Reconciliation

*R*ECALL THAT PRIOR *to being sent to Hong Kong for medical treatment in 1980, Dominic Tang was appointed bishop of Canton by the Bureau of Religious Affairs. The following year in Rome he was appointed archbishop of Guangzhou (Canton). Observers, perceiving the Vatican appointment to be in harmony with the Chinese government appointment, saw in Bishop Tang a bridge. However, the reaction in Peking, where the announcement was viewed as an attempt to meddle in Chinese affairs and establish the supremacy of the pope, was violent; hopes of establishing a bridge between the Vatican and Peking were all but extinguished.*

A bridge between the Chinese government and Chinese Catholics is what the Chinese Catholic Patriotic Association (CCPA) professes to be. Father Wong was in close contact with one of its leaders, Aloysius Luxian Jin, who was ordained as bishop in 1985. Like many other

priests, Jin was arrested in Shanghai on September 8, 1955. Following
his arrest, the broadcast of his tape-recorded message urging Catholics
to support the government was considered a betrayal by many includ-
ing Margaret Chu, the niece of Bishop Kung Pin-mei. On the same day
in 1960, both Jin and Kung were sentenced to prison. Kung (he was ele-
vated to cardinal, in pectore, in 1979, though it was only announced to
the world in 1991; since 1987 he has resided in the United States) was
sentenced to twenty years (some reports say that he was given a life sen-
tence), while Jin received only eighteen years because, it is claimed, he
was willing to reveal the crimes of others. However, there is no hard evi-
dence that Jin named anyone to his or her detriment.

Father Wong urges generous consideration of Bishop Jin. Rather than
condemn him for assuming leadership in the CCPA, Father Wong
would have overseas Catholics look at the good that is coming from his
work in the public church and at the seminary. The suggestion is that
since the full story is unknown, it would be better to consider his actions
as sincere and judge them by their fruits. Catholics outside mainland
China are called to be a bridge between the public and underground
churches, offering love and compassion to both sides.

✧   ✧   ✧

SEVERAL PAGES BACK I described how I simultaneously celebrated Mass in the catacombs of Shanghai, remaining in contact
and communion with my underground confrères and refusing the
overtures of the Patriotic Association, while I taught English at the
seminary operated by the Patriotics. You may recall that I also served
as personal secretary to the episcopal rector in the public church. I
know that my position puzzles some people. On the one hand, I was
in close association with (underground) Bishop Peter Joseph Fan
(Xue-yan), who was ordained with me in 1951, and on the other
hand, I was in close contact with (public) Bishop Aloysius Jin Luxian,

who was present at our ordination. It is understandable that people might be confused by what seems a contradiction: my refusal to align myself with the public church and yet work in their seminary and for their bishop.

As for my position about this complex situation, I will start by attempting to make my view clear: there is one universal church headed up by Peter's successor. This is an absolute, and any other model is schismatic. I am willing to acknowledge that things change over time, even within the universal church. Our Lord calls us to read the signs of the times, and St. Ignatius built into the Constitutions of the Society of Jesus an openness to change, announcing to future Jesuits that they may be called to adapt the Constitutions to other times and cultures while remaining faithful to the church and ready to serve in the vineyard of the Lord.

Sometimes caught up in a delicate balancing act, we are called to discernment as we ask for light to be shed on murky and troubling issues. But discernment begins with trust in God, who works mysteriously and, by our timetables, perhaps slowly. In trusting God and by accepting that things don't necessarily happen how and when we want, we are able to submit to God's holy will. In the middle of the eighteenth century a papal bull condemned the Chinese Rites, setting back the work done by the early Jesuit missionaries who had sought to understand and adapt to the Chinese, distinguishing between the absolutes in Christianity and accidents of culture. Let us not forget that our Jesuits, caught up in their enthusiasm for their work, ignored repeated requests from Rome to defend the Chinese Rites. So be it. Two hundred years later the church repealed the denunciation of the Chinese Rites, and nowadays we find ourselves encouraging the faithful to seek Christ in diverse cultures.

Ours is an organic church, constantly praying, constantly going through her own examen of consciousness, and constantly growing in grace and wisdom. Just as for an individual, this growth must, nevertheless, come from within—in this case, from within the church—not from without. Change must find its source in the love of Christ and the body of believers, not fear or governmental mandate. How confident are the words of St. Paul, who proclaims that "neither death nor life, nor angels, nor principalities, nothing already in existence and nothing still to come, nor any power, nor the heights nor the depths, nor any created thing whatever, will be able to come between us and the love of God, known to us in Christ Jesus our Lord" (Romans 8:38–39). Faith, love, and obedience are what keep us unified and strong.

Still, Our Lord told Peter to feed his lambs. In China we find multitudes of spiritually hungry faithful flocking to churches with genuine fervor. Providing them with a way to practice their faith and educating seminarians so that they might be good shepherds—in my case, making a small contribution by teaching English so that they could communicate with the faithful throughout the world—is doing the Lord's work. Demonstrating against the religious services conducted under the auspices of the Patriotic Association is not. Making noise outside the public churches as the faithful inside lift their voices to make a joyful noise unto the Lord is rude and hateful. Rejoicing that illness caused the pope to postpone his trip to visit seminarians in New York, including some from the ranks of the Chinese Patriotics, and therefore would not be able to offer them his blessing does not fit with my view of being Christlike. Being quick to criticize and accuse, especially when love is not the primary motivator, is not helpful in building the kingdom.

An example of the growth within the church is the call to be ecumenical. I personally was very impressed by an editorial that appeared in the September 22, 1979, issue of *America*. I was able to read back issues of the magazine that had been forwarded to my brother, Willie, who kept them for me to peruse after my final release and retirement from White Lake Farm in 1983. In this particular write-up, John O'Hare, S.J., spoke of a glorious moment in St. Patrick's Cathedral in New York when Terence Cardinal Cooke conducted a religious service in the sanctuary alongside the Dalai Lama and an unnamed Protestant minister. As Buddhist monks chanted, the Dalai Lama threw some rice into the air as a gesture of thanksgiving for the grain and for sustenance. The Protestant minister offered reflections on St. Paul's hymn to charity from the first letter to the Corinthians. There were also readings from the Talmud by rabbis from New York. Mayor Edward Koch was present with his rabbi. Cardinal Cooke explained that while we all treasure our own religious traditions and can't pretend to form some new, universal religion, we can pray together and seek to share our common values. For him to be flanked in the sanctuary by a Buddhist and a Protestant represented an edifying lesson in ecumenism; my teaching English in a seminary operated under the auspices of the Patriotic Association was little by comparison, but it was done in the same spirit and does not for one minute indicate a disloyalty to the Holy See.

As for those who have joined up with the public church, we have to be generous and lenient. Frankly, we do not know what is going on in their hearts; it is between themselves and God. While I was still in China, it was my understanding that at least 60 percent of so-called public bishops were actually in secret union with Rome; I think the number is closer to 80 percent today. The most widely known of the public bishops is Bishop Aloysius Jin Luxian. As a Chinese Jesuit, he graduated from the Gregorian, from the Pontifical University in Rome, and spent time studying in Germany as well. He speaks French, German, Italian, English, and, of course, Chinese. Prior to his twenty-year imprisonment, Father Jin had been rector at the seminary. After his release, he found himself in a heartrending dilemma as the Patriotic Association, recognizing his talents and experience, asked him to resume the rectorship of the seminary they planned to open; then they would ask him to serve as bishop.

It seems to me that he made the right choice in accepting to be rector of the seminary. There, students can get a good education as they attend the lectures of great theologians visiting from all over the world—professors like Jesuit Father Edward Malatesta, one of Father Frank's protégés who was, until his sudden death in 1998, director of the Ricci Institute for Chinese-Western Cultural History at the University of San Francisco, where he continued the work of our mentor. Certainly none of us in China had any current knowledge or experience regarding the church; the visiting professors, able to offer our Chinese students new, rich insights, contribute to helping the Chinese stay more in step with the universal church throughout the world. And the students have the privilege of studying abroad. Rather than create division, these exchanges promote unity.

The decision to accept the office of bishop was more difficult for Jin. Now, I know that Bishop Jin sought consultation on this matter from the underground hierarchy, but his request for a meeting was refused. The easy thing to do is resort to the polemic of one side being right and one being wrong, or one side seeking understanding and counsel and the other remaining rigid. However, a generous imagination leads to other scenarios. Perhaps the underground leaders did not want to influence Father Jin's decision; perhaps they did not want to put themselves in a compromising position. Perhaps they understood that the crucifixion precedes the resurrection. One way to look at the situation is to understand that Bishop Jin may be hurting deeply to be perceived as the public betrayer of those who suffered for their loyalty to the church. He has opened himself to vicious criticism and gossip about his past history and his character.

There was another Chinese Jesuit, who has since died, who during the Cultural Revolution weakened in fear and denied his faith. As soon as he stepped on the crucifix, his heart was filled with painful remorse, and I can guarantee you that he regretted the rest of his life that moment of weakness that spared him the brutal treatment of the People's Republic but gave him no peace. Many years later I asked a confrère to join me in making a visit to this priest, who had fallen sick. It grieves me deeply that my confrère refused, saying the sick priest wasn't worth a visit since he had desecrated the crucifix. But what about Our Lord's example? Was not Peter guilty of denying his Master? He wept copiously and bitterly as the cock crowed. And Christ made him the head of the church. There must never be any prohibition for a fallen-away priest to repent and come back to the church.

Our Lord gave us another example in his parable about the prodigal son which, more a story about how a father loved his son than about how a son changed his ways, teaches us about reconciliation. What we are called to do is open the channels of communication, forgive generously, and prepare the banquet to celebrate our reconciliation even when we are distraught by terrible things that seem to make no sense—as in March of 1997 when underground Bishop Joseph Fan's quarters were ransacked by the police and his Bible, rosary, and money confiscated. We cannot let these acts keep us divided, for the Holy Father calls us to this unity. We must pray that the bridge church of the diaspora of overseas Chinese Catholics will play a decisive role in attaining the ideal of one Lord, one faith, one church.

Our faith invites us to let Christ's love heal the wounds we suffered rather than to foster alienation by fighting on behalf of the pope. There is a Chinese saying for those who, though with sincere intentions, would defend the Holy See to an undesirable and unhealthy— that is, nonsalvific—extreme: *Yue bang yue mang,* which translates, "The more you help, the more you hinder." There is a Western saying as well: "To be more Catholic than the pope." Let us not hinder the Holy Father but work with him toward reconciliation.

❖ 23 ❖

Bamboo Swaying
in the Wind

*T*HERE ARE MILLIONS *of overseas Chinese Catholics. One large Chinese Catholic community meets for the Sunday liturgy in Chinese at St. Clare's Church in Santa Clara, California. The parents join other adults in the main church, but they send their children to the vast room in the church basement for Mass in English. Scores of youngsters ranging in age from three years to the teen years attend. Up until very recently, Father Wong regularly presided at the children's Mass. The teens, members of the Watermark Youth Group, actually prepare and direct the liturgy, informing their brothers and sisters about when to stand, leading them in song, offering the prayers of the faithful, and taking their hands during the Our Father. Young children participate actively as well; even tiny tots listen attentively to the homily and respond* *spontaneously to particular points by nodding their little heads yes or no. It is no wonder that they were comfortable climbing onto Father Wong's lap at his birthday celebration.*

Since 1939, the church has taken a broader view of the tradition of ancestor veneration. Interestingly, little has been done inside China to develop this rite, while Chinese-American parishes have found it attractive both for recent immigrants and for American-born Chinese. At St. Mary's Cathedral in San Francisco, for example, the Chinese New Year Mass includes special offerings and prayers for ancestors, connecting the faithful with the cloud of witnesses. This kind of rite is appreciated by others, not only the Chinese, in a church that is blessed by the Communion of Saints. It is one example of inculturation now being practiced in California parishes by the grandchildren and great-grandchildren of those who welcomed the California Jesuits to China sixty years ago.

✣   ✣   ✣

A T THE BEGINNING of my story I explained how the Chinese count birth from conception. When I turned seventy-nine by Western standards, the Chinese community of the diocese of San Jose organized my eightieth birthday party. This gala celebration took place in the parish hall of St. Clare's Church in Santa Clara, California. Ellen Yang, elegant and charming and energetic, was the mistress of ceremonies with about two hundred people in attendance, including my nephew Eddie and his children; Betty Crighton Lee, who had come from New York; and Sister Mary Celeste Rouleau, Father Rouleau's niece.

I was deeply moved by the manifestation of their love. Delicious, piping hot Chinese delicacies were served for dinner; guests had their choice of chopsticks or forks and knives. And there was a birthday cake with so many candles that I thought that we might need the fire brigade; at the very least, I was grateful for the help of many young-sters in blowing the candles out. It was a joyful occasion, and the merriment included beautiful singing. The gracious voices of Taiwanese Sisters Teresa and Regina, the latter playing the guitar, filled the room as they sang "Peace in My Heart," and Father Gregory Kimm's rendition of "Love Is Here to Stay" warmed the hearts of everyone in the room. Father Frank would have said that we were having a wild, hilarious time. And then we heard "God Bless You" sung in Cantonese and "Salve Regina" in Latin.

One of the highlights of the evening was the living rosary. Taken to a seat in the front of the room, I observed that the people had joined hands to form a large ring around the room. They became the beads of a living rosary, and cross bearer Kenneth Wang, chairman of the Chinese community, led the Creed in Mandarin. Passing a can-dle among them, Father Matthew Koo said the Our Father in Mandarin, Father James Chevedden said the first Hail Mary in Mandarin, Father Augustine Tsang said the second in Cantonese, and Father Gregory Kimm, the only priest there who wasn't a Jesuit, said the third in English.

As the beads of the living rosary moved at each decade, I found myself face to face first with the faith-sharing group of the Chinese community, all dressed in red and reciting in Mandarin, and then with the Cantonese group, who, in green, did the second decade. High school and university students from the Watermark Youth Group, the blue of their shirts and denim jeans having transformed them into Marian messengers, recited the third decade in English, and then they moved on to make way for the fourth decade said in Mandarin by members of the Legion of Mary wearing red garments. Finally, in green, came the people from the Bible-study group; they recited the fifth decade in Mandarin. In this timeless moment I saw a living chain bound by love and devotion and stronger than any chain used to hobble prisoners or keep their hands tied behind their back.

As if that were not enough, there were many presents, starting with the display of artwork as little children climbed up into my lap. Among the masterpieces was their scroll on which brush strokes had formed graceful branches and crepe paper had made delicate blossoms. As for me, I saw God's handiwork in their joyful countenances; in the eagerness with which the teenagers offered happy songs, inviting the whole congregation to join in; and in the cross they had made for me and in the symbol of the Holy Spirit, a reminder of Gladys Wei and the Sisters of Social Service, which they pinned to my lapel. I mused that long ago I had willingly given up my liberty, understanding, memory, and will—though I was a little surprised that Our Lord had taken me so seriously about my memory, which indeed seems to be fading—finding his grace and love enough for me. Truly my cup was full and running over with grace and love that night.

As we grow in grace and wisdom and age, we like to recapture the exuberance of youth. One of my birthday cards bore the Chinese saying, *Xiao-xio: shi-nien sho,* which translates into English as "Each time you laugh makes you ten years younger." To laugh or to smile is depicted in written Chinese by the picture of bamboo. It is said that a person rocking with laughter looks like bamboo swaying in the wind; it suggests happiness too. Laughing makes us happy, healthy, and strong like bamboo. The Ninetieth Psalm also talks about grass springing up in the morning when it flowers and withering and fading in the evening. We are told that our span is seventy years or eighty for those who are strong. I am grateful that I have been strong like bamboo for these eighty years.

St. Ignatius of Loyola knew about laughing and swaying in the wind like bamboo. Praying as he did for generosity, I have tried to live my life accordingly:

> Lord, teach me to be generous.
> Teach me to serve you as you deserve;
> To give and not to count the cost,
> To fight and not to heed the wounds,

To toil and not to seek for rest,
To labor and not to ask for reward,
Save that of knowing that I do your will.

At that birthday celebration I could see Christ's family growing in wisdom and grace, two hundred people whose lives have been touched by the young man who encountered Father Frank almost sixty years before. Swaying in the wind—how rich these years have been, and how very fast they have gone by!

At the canonization of Claude La Colombière, Rome, 1992.

Following canonization of Claude La Colombière, Rome, 1992.
With Father Wong and the Holy Father are Jesuits John Vessels,
Secretary General, Apostleship of Prayer; Paolo Molinari,
Postulator General; and Father General Peter-Hans Kolvenbach.

George Wong, S.J., on vacation in Puerto Vallarta, Mexico, 1996, where he told Claudia Devaux much of his story.

Father Wong's eightieth birthday party, with children, 1997.

Father Wong preaching at St. Clare's Church in Santa Clara, 1993.

Father Wong, 1994.

⁑ afterword ⁑

Heaven endures; Earth lasts a long time.
The reason why Heaven and Earth can endure and last a long time
Is that they do not live for themselves.
Therefore they can endure.

Therefore the Sage:
Puts himself in the background, yet finds himself in the foreground;
Puts self-concern out of his mind, yet finds that his self-concern is
    preserved.
Is it not because he has no self-interest,
That he is therefore able to realize his self-interest?

My first encounter with Father Wong took place in 1994 when I was writing a paper on Chinese rituals and was specifically interested in the relationship between Chinese ancestral ceremonies and the Communion of Saints. Little did I know that our meeting would not be a simple interview about Eastern and Western practices; instead it was the beginning of an experience. He invited me that day to the Mass he was celebrating for the children of the Chinese community and, on another occasion, to the ordination of four Jesuit priests, one of them from China.

Told later that Father Wong had a mental block concerning his imprisonment, I was dumbfounded, since our lively conversations covered a full range of topics, including his prison experience. Love, peace, joy, and hope seemed to emanate from this man, who might have been bitter or cynical. Sensing that I was in the presence of a mystic, I felt somewhat like the seeker approaching the sage to ask about the secrets of life. But there would be no direct answers to specific questions, only a story that would unfold in a loving partnership as we walked and talked together. It is a story about living in the present, about being open to grace, about seeing signs and connections as manifestations of God's love. As for the secrets, I shall attempt to share them as they were revealed to me.

First and foremost comes the conviction that people are inherently good. Starting his life as a scholar, *Hua Quan,* the Little Flower, learned the calligraphic strokes proclaiming in the words of Mencius that man, at the beginning, seeks goodness. Now, Father Wong did not spontaneously volunteer this recollection of his early days as a scholar. Rather, I asked him about the first words he learned to write, and in recalling the proclamation of Mencius, he admitted that the sound had made more of an impression on him than the meaning. Still, as our conversation continued, it became evident that the meaning was printed on the heart of this man, whose life reflects his belief that all people naturally seek goodness even if their "business" gets in the way.

Once, when I was giving a talk on Asian manufacturing practices, I brought up these words of Mencius. An attendee at the conference suggested a bit critically that this saying differed from the Christian concept of original sin. Perhaps there is ambiguity, but I do not believe that the two are mutually exclusive ideas. In the Spiritual Exercises, Ignatius of Loyola, acknowledging evil in the world, uses the imagination to the point of seeing fire, hearing shrieking, feeling pain, tasting bitterness, and smelling suffering (*SpEx* 66–70), but he also encourages the opposite view, as described in the Genesis account, that what God has created is good—the saints, the heavens, the sun, moon, and stars, the elements, the fruits, birds, fishes, and animals (*SpEx* 60). Ignatius would have us understand that God created people for love and service, that is, he created them good.

The Presupposition of the Spiritual Exercises (*SpEx* 22), in calling for a favorable interpretation to be put on another's statement, is grounded in the idea that people are created good. The first thing is to be willing to accept the other as sincere; if there is reason to doubt what the other is saying, then it is necessary to look for a misinterpretation and to clear it up. During his regency, short though it was because of the impending Communist takeover, the young Jesuit would have an example in Father Farmer, who "was always kind in his criticism; he never called anyone a piker or a fool, although, separating the actor from the act, he referred sometimes to mistakes as foolish."

Time and again Father Wong has manifested his readiness to offer the benefit of the doubt to others; one significant example is in the case of the public church. His refusal to join the Patriotic Association responsible for overseeing the administration of the public church in China resulted in his being sent back to the labor camp in 1981. Nevertheless, Father Wong is supportive of the seminary at Zosé, where he taught English, he is pleased that people flock to the reopened churches to worship together, and he suggests that we judge public Bishop Aloysius Luxian Jin by the fruits of his labor, since we cannot know what is in his heart.

For Father Wong, sincerity in seeking God is the key to salvation, superseding any profession of faith. What stands out in his memory of the telegraph operator is the man's purity of heart. Lengthy doctrinal explanations were not possible, and so Father Wong's focusing on his cell mate's sincerity as he prepared to baptize him reminds us of the words of Jesus that whoever humbles himself like a child is the greatest in the kingdom of heaven (Matthew 18:4) and the words of

Mencius that the great man does not lose his childlike heart.[2] Delighted to welcome a newcomer into the church, Father Wong nevertheless believed then, as he does now, in the "baptism of desire."

As he completed his theology studies, he prepared a thesis arguing that salvation was available to those outside the church; today Father Wong takes great comfort in the fourth Eucharistic prayer that asks God to remember all those who seek him with a sincere heart. Likewise, Confucian teachings include consideration of the sincerity of individuals making sacrifices on behalf of their ancestors. When one scholar, Chu Hsi, was asked whether sacrifices of wine, meat, and silk were merely to express sincerity or whether some force actually came to receive the sacrifice, he answered that there was no point in having the sacrifice if nothing came of it, but that to say that a spirit came riding in a chariot was just wild talk.[3] Reminded that Ignatius did not approve of talk about extraordinary phenomena,[4] I point out that what Chu Hsi was getting at was a continuity between the one offering the sacrifice and the object of the sacrifice based on sincerity of the will.[5] Confucius's pupil Tseng Tzu taught that sincerity in the individual was the beginning of peace in the world:

> When one's will becomes sincere, the mind is rectified,
> when the mind is rectified, the personal life is cultivated;
> when the personal life is cultivated, the family will be regulated;
> when the family is regulated, the state will be in order;
> and, when the state is in order, there will be peace throughout the
>   world.[6]

Life in this world with all its connections constitutes Father Wong's ontology, and yet it all starts with the individual. A similar verse demonstrates again that even a tradition as occupied with society as Confucianism teaches:

> If there be righteousness in the heart, there will be beauty in the
>   character.
> If there be beauty in the character, there will be harmony in the
>   home.

If there be harmony in the home, there will be order in the nation.

If there be order in the nation, there will be peace in the world.[7]

Hearing Christ's exhortation to seek first the kingdom of God, we are told that the kingdom of God is within us (Luke 17:21). Our Christian heritage would have us emulate him in emptying ourselves (Philippians 2:7) and thereby make way for righteousness, peace, and joy in the Holy Spirit (Romans 14:17). The Philippian hymn proclaims that Christ did not count equality with God as something to be grasped at but that he emptied himself and took the form of a slave in becoming human (Philippians 2:6–7). Humbling ourselves at the Eucharist, we express our unworthiness ("I am not worthy, Lord, but only say the word, and I shall be healed") in much the same way that we hear the Chinese gentleman refer to himself as "this coarse and illiterate person" and are reminded that we are not loved by God because we are lovable but because God is Love.[8]

Indifference, that is, an emptying of preferences, is the whole foundation and principle supporting the Spiritual Exercises (*SpEx* 53). In order to know, love, and serve God and to recognize and appreciate grace, we need to keep ourselves indifferent and not be led by our likes and dislikes, even in matters of health or sickness, wealth or poverty, or whether we are living in the East or in the West.

Raised in a Buddhist household, Father Wong had an appreciation for the idea of suffering brought on by desire and strife and for the freedom that comes with indifference, that is, detachment:

The perfect way knows no difficulties

Except that it refuses to make preferences. . . .

If you wish to see it before your own eyes

Have no fixed thoughts either for or against it.[9]

When we think of sin and suffering in the world, we probably do not imagine starting with ourselves, nor do we realize how liberating holy indifference can be. Ridding oneself of preferences may be as simple as relaxing and letting go of opinions, according to Buddhist

Scripture: "Try not to seek after the true/Only cease to cherish opinions."[10] To those doing the Spiritual Exercises, Ignatius suggests seeking the intercession of the Blessed Mother in order to understand the disorder in one's life (*SpEx* 63). Ignatius has the exercitants imagine a scene where the Persons of the Trinity are looking at the suffering on earth, and then he asks that they contemplate the response of Mary to God's messenger Gabriel (*SpEx* 102–103). Totally surrendering herself to the will of God, she provides an example of perfect receptivity. "You see before you the Lord's servant. Let it happen to me" (Luke 1:38). She is at once an intercessor and a model of humility.

Father Wong places great trust in the Blessed Mother, whom he cannot bring himself to call Mary, except when saying the Hail Mary, so deep is his respect for her. Once, when he was a bit anxious about meeting friends for dinner, I surprised myself by suggesting that he put the matter into Our Lady's hands; later he told me that my advice was right on the mark. By letting her take over his concern, he was able to focus on the present and to move closer to God. Through *wu-wei,* or actionless action, the Blessed Mother brings the individual to the Father.

Though in solitary confinement in a Shanghai prison, Father Wong was never alone, for he would feel the presence of Our Lady. In contrast, many who live in society are sadly alienated. The Blessed Mother has a Chinese counterpart whose picture appeared on a bookmark that Father Wong sent to me. She is *Kuan-yin,* the madonna-like goddess of mercy in Chinese Buddhism. Always ready to hear the prayers of the world and bless people with the willow branch in her vase, she is a model of actionless action. Representing being-in-compassion, she refuses to enter nirvana until all sentient beings are saved.

His own integration of the yin and the yang, the anima and the animus, the feminine and the masculine, is central to Father Wong's spirituality. Helping him achieve this healthy balance along his life journey was his friendship with Gladys Wei. Reminiscing, Father Wong would refer to this relationship as the divine romance of two

vocations. Yes, it was a romance, but more than that, it was a friendship that would have received the blessing of the nineteenth-century
French philosopher Joseph Joubert, who, in a period charged with
romanticism, wryly suggested that one should only choose for a wife
the woman one would choose if she were a man.[11] Both George Wong
and Gladys Wei had Western names (his was given to him by the husband—a British subject who was a Freemason and a Protestant—of
a woman he called his aunt; she chose hers because she liked the
sound of "glad" in it), they had been educated in Catholic schools,
and they shared a deep piety.

The young man was delighted to find in Gladys a kindred spirit
interested in the same books and magazines, but he was confused
about why she declined his offer to accompany him to see a Cecil B.
DeMille film. And then he was devastated when she sent him a letter
breaking off all contact between them. He blamed himself for somehow offending her delicacy. Fortunately, his mentor, Father Francis
Rouleau, patched things up between them, although even as an elderly
man, Father Wong would remain puzzled about what he had said or
done to offend Gladys. I suggested that perhaps the impetus to curtail
the relationship had nothing to do with him and everything to do
with herself and her own confusion. Father replied, "Could be, could
be." Later, when I returned from a visit with Sister Bertille Prus, who
shared her novitiate days with Gladys Wei (Sister Candida in religious
life) and who nursed her during her final illness, Father Wong was
pleased to learn of the support for my theory. "She was a feisty one,"
exclaimed Sister Bertille, and Father Wong admitted that with Gladys
there was "no monkey business or halfway vocation."

Their apostolates were a reflection of complementary natures.
Gladys may have been delicate and fragile, and yet she was a woman
of action. Members of her religious community remember her as the
tiny sister standing on a stool at the kitchen sink and passing the
dishes to be dried so quickly that they called her "the China clipper."
They tell of their bewilderment at finding her patiently unraveling

the sweater that she had told them she was going to wash. She did wash the wool and then, needles flying, knitted the sweater anew; that was the Chinese way.

In Shanghai, Sister Candida organized and led a boys' club, a mothers' club, and a teen choir, managing to make the Cantonese members feel comfortable with the Shanghai members. She taught English to adults. Before the Communist takeover, she used her family connections to arrange meetings with the mayor and other officials in order to assure that relief goods were properly distributed. When a relief package arrived from overseas with clothes too fancy and impractical for the intended recipients, she had her sewing group use the fabric to make padded jackets. The Sisters of Social Service were a progressive order. They wore uniforms instead of habits, and they did not travel in pairs but got around in their own jeep or by pedicab. Father Wong was busy in his own way, but his work was more structured and dealt with the spiritual matters of Mass, devotions, and confessions. Her ministry was closely associated with the earth (yin) and his with heaven (yang), though they shared a common *tao* ("way"). Tearfully, he told me that when news of Gladys's death reached him, he longed to switch places with her so that she could continue her ministry of good works.

Gladys's letter served an important purpose in Father Wong's life. It wounded him, forcing him to turn in upon himself. Unable to eat or sleep, Father Wong felt his own anguish. Later he would be asked to consider Christ suffering in his humanity (*SpEx* 195), to ponder the hiding divinity (*SpEx* 196), and to imagine Christ descending to the Valley of Josephat (*SpEx* 201). He would be asked to pray for the gift of being able to feel sorrow with Christ, to be anguished with Christ's anguish, and to experience tears and deep grief (*SpEx* 203). This is not to compare his wound with the wounds of Christ but to propose that the intensity of his own experience enabled him to receive the gift of feeling sorrow and anguish with Christ. In his personal trip to the valley, he was put in touch with the feminine qualities of human existence that let him share the wounds and suffering of others and yet remain hopeful. In fact, using his own experience for reference, he advised me, as I was about to embark on the Long Retreat, not to be afraid of tears but to welcome them and embrace them, for they would bring consolation:

> When you know the male yet hold on to the female,
> You'll be the ravine of the country.
> When you're the ravine of the country,
> Your constant virtue will not leave.
> And when your constant virtue doesn't leave,
> You'll return to the state of the infant.[12]

Returning to the state of the infant can be taken to mean becoming whole and wise. Confucius did not identify the poles of an individual's life as masculine and feminine, but he did teach the embracing of the mean as a way to wholeness and wisdom. Using the metaphor of the Knight of the Way who takes on the burden of humanity (*jen*), the great Sage tells us that steering the middle course is the only way for the Knight to realize himself, and yet few have been able to follow it consistently "if just for one round month."[13] What the Knight of the Way must do is "set his heart on the Way," broaden himself with culture (*wen*), and refine himself with ritual (*li*). The journey is never over, and a man is always in the process of becoming himself. Like other priests in prison, Father Wong would renew himself through the Spiritual Exercises, taking "one round month" to make his retreat each year under the guidance of the Holy Spirit.

Confucius did not actually describe the qualities of caring, forgiving, and accepting as feminine, but his followers have as they note the suggestion of receptivity.[14] Engendered by a spirit of detachment, these are the qualities that enable a silent appreciation of the world. For Confucius to rid himself of opinions and dogma required long and strenuous self-examination. So important to Ignatius was the daily Examen of Conscience (*SpEx* 27–43) that he made it the one prayer never to be preempted when carrying out the work of the Lord.

Even before Father Wong had heard that in today's language we use the term Examen of Consciousness to emphasize the personal awareness of continual renewal, he understood that Ignatius intended for his followers to do more than correct faults. He saw that salvation was the work of a lifetime rather than the result of a decision or promise made in a single moment (*SpEx* 367). Prayer and reflection enable the individual to practice virtue and cultivate the good in order to grow like Jesus in grace and wisdom before God (Luke 2:40). Ignatian prayer always includes placing oneself before God, and that can mean letting go of opinions, dogma, and distractions.

At one point in the Spiritual Exercises, the individual is called to a deeper response to the mysteries of Christ's life (*SpEx* 120). In prison, Father Wong fashioned a rosary out of a rag, using five knots to contemplate Christ's life on earth. Prior to this he had trained all his senses to respond in a passive way; he used the imagination to contemplate persons coming into contact with the Lord, to see them and hear what they were saying, to smell and taste the fragrance of divinity and of the soul and its virtues, and to touch and kiss the places where those being contemplated had been (*SpEx* 121–126). Such silent appreciation of the world, another example of *wu-wei,* or actionless action, Ignatius called "the Application of the senses."

Father Wong manifests his appreciation of the world and his connection to it in many ways. Standing in St. Mary's Cathedral following his concelebration of an evening Mass, he gazed out the window overlooking San Francisco, in awe of the city lights. And so we toured the city, looking back at the illuminated cathedral from Twin Peaks and then stopping for hot chocolate at a coffeehouse on Irving Street. It was on that occasion that he told me about the failure of acupuncture, administered by amateurs, to relieve the pain of his appendectomy at the labor camp. Laughing, and yet totally serious in seeing the whole affair as a blessing, he added that he did not suffer from any aftereffects of anesthesia.

Another time, Father Wong thoroughly enjoyed the San Francisco exhibition of Chinese art, featuring treasures from the National Palace Museum in Taipei. That pleasant day, our conversation was about perspective and vast spaces between tiny trees and gigantic cliffs, cursive calligraphy, puzzle boxes, and the realistic horses of Jesuit missionary Giuseppe Castiglione (1688–1766), whose complex style perfectly suited Emperor Ch'ien-lung. At the Ricci Institute, where we reviewed four hundred 35-mm slides catalogued by the late Peter Joseph Fleming—the last slides in the set were of Father Wong—he marveled at the work started by his mentor Father Francis Rouleau and continued by Father Edward Malatesta, who greeted us there.

Intrigued by the computer technology enabling communication with scholars all over the world, he delighted in the graphics on the screen and the music coming from the speakers. Joining my husband and me at our evening ritual of watching the sunset in Puerto Vallarta, Father quoted Francis Thompson's "Ode to the Orient," with special reference to "the flaming monstrance of the West." My artistic ambition of videotaping him walking pensively along the beach with his hands behind his back and the sun setting in the background was foiled—I had intended to superimpose the recitation of the poem on the videotape—because instead of reflecting somberly, he trotted merrily, speaking to children and waving to all with a big grin on his face. This is the man who waded through rice paddies in the scorching sun as leeches attacked his legs—the wounds remain— and who at night secretly presided at the Lord's table. As his *laogai* companions slept in the dormitory, he was in touch with the whole universal church. A simple ritual with simple gifts of bread and wine that he could see, smell, touch, and taste as the consecration bell sounded in his memory, it was both a mystical union with God and a communion with the body of Christ.

In prison, there would be other connections with the body of Christ. There was the Christmas hymn sung soulfully by the

Frenchman and the gift of wine in the penicillin bottle from the doctor in the *laogai* camp. Humbled, with his hands manacled behind his back, Father Wong accepted the help of his cell mate, coincidentally or providentially a former student, in eating and with his personal hygiene. The song, the wine, the sponge on his back in the hot summer were gifts of love received with a gratitude akin to that of Jesus when the woman appeared with her alabaster jar at the supper in Bethany (Matthew 26:6–10; *SpEx* 286). Ignatius, teaching that love consists of a mutual sharing of goods and gifts, recommends the cultivation of gratitude (*SpEx* 230–237). The sun pours out its rays and the fountain its waters as God pours himself out. Every day for the past sixty years, Father has recited the Suscipe, or "Take and Receive" prayer (*SpEx* 234), offering everything—liberty, memory, will—to God, asking only for his love and grace in return. For Father Wong, this was not just a private prayer, as he was conscious of saying the words with tens of thousands of Jesuits all over the world.

Partly because of him and certainly thanks to him, I make it a point to join my faith community not just for Mass during the day but for the Liturgy of the Hours. The harmonious recitation of the psalms and canticles helps me focus and remember to breathe in a world that is otherwise feverish and frantic; moreover, it means that I am praying with the church. Just how deep this connection can be was demonstrated to me when Father Wong joined us for morning prayer. Aware that age is taking its toll, he had mused about the Lord's taking very seriously the offering of his memory since he finds himself frequently searching for the right word. More frail now, he gets confused and forgetful. However, that morning as we walked into the chapel for the Liturgy of the Hours, Father announced confidently, "So it's Monday morning of week three." Ignatius instructs us to praise and reverence the sacramental life of the church and the prayer life of the church especially in the Eucharist and in the Divine Office (*SpEx* 354–355).

Confucius believed that poetry was a guide for harmonizing human emotions, stimulating the mind, teaching the art of sociality, and showing how to regulate feelings of resentment. He considered a person always to be a center of relationships rather than a separate individual complete in himself or herself; it is through ritual that one learns to be human as a part of a community with others.[15] Besides being in harmony with the universal church and his fellow Jesuits, Father Wong takes delight in relationships. The baptism of his own father brought consolation to the future priest, not because it was a requirement for entry into heaven but because it united the senior Wong with the rest of the family.

The day of our visit to the Ricci Institute, Father Wong took a nap after lunch at the Jesuit residence. I offered to pick him up later, but he insisted that he would "sponge a ride" and meet me at the institute, so I figured that he would ask one of his confrères for transportation. In the afternoon, he walked into the Ricci Institute, smiling and telling me how a nice Mexican family had brought him up the hill in their car. "Did you know them?" I asked. He answered that he had simply flagged them down, assuming that they were Catholic, and they were happy to oblige. Though he did not say so, I am sure that he gave them his blessing and that it was graciously accepted.

Another time, he found the complications of applying for a visa to Hong Kong suddenly removed after he had spoken to a sympathetic agent. "I wonder if she was Catholic," he queried. This seemed to him the logical explanation for the favorable change in procedures. In Mexico, where he concelebrated Mass, the universal family was once again brought together as prayers were offered by the faithful there for the church in China. In fact, the first time I met Father Wong, he told me that even though he did not know me then, he was praying for me while he was in prison; for my part, I remembered the conversation I had with my grandmother as a small child curious about "the different tongue" of the people in China.

At our first meeting, Father also commented with delight on the relationship between my name, Claudia, and that of Claude La Colombière, whose canonization Mass he concelebrated with Pope John Paul II. The connections of Father Wong's universal family transcend time and space. He sensed the prayers of Gladys Wei and her devotion to the Holy Spirit when his handcuffs were removed after fifty days and nights; that is the same length of time as between Easter and the descent of the Holy Spirit at Pentecost. He takes great consolation in the Communion of Saints as he shares his prayers with Father Rouleau.

Being required to sign and date depositions that were used in his interrogations, as well as read newspapers full of propaganda, was a blessing for Father Wong in prison. The rays of sun entering his prison cell proclaimed God's love (*SpEx* 237), and their position told him the time as did the ringing of the Angelus when we were in Mexico. In prison, the dates of the newspapers kept him in touch with the calendar, and so he was able to remember feast days and to share in celebrations with the family that makes up the church. This now makes me especially sensitive to observing the traditional feast days, so easily cast aside, as I imagine myself praying with many people, in prison or not, throughout the world. St. Paul writes that the cup that we bless is a sharing in the blood of Christ and that we, though many, share in the one loaf (1 Corinthians 10:16–17).

In Chinese tradition, ancestors and descendents share not only common blood but also the same material force. The continuity of a family can be compared to the sea, with each generation a different wave. One wave is not realized without the other's being fully realized, and just as the wave behind affects the wave in front, people offering sacrifices to ancestors can affect them.[16] Likewise the moon, though its light is scattered on lakes and rivers, is not split.[17] And Christ is wholly present in the broken bread, shared now and in past and future generations, giving us eternal life now in the present.

Ours is a church of history with temporal instruments—the liturgy and the whole sacramental system—that enable God's grace to come to us and make contact with the eternal.[18] Ignatius would have us reverence those who have gone before us, offering prayers for their support while recognizing our devotion as living out the mystery of the Communion of Saints (*SpEx* 358). And like the ancient Chinese, Ignatius would have us, out of filial respect, not offend the God who loves us (*SpEx* 370). George Bernard Wong, leaving for California to enter the Society of Jesus in 1939, was impressed by Father Rouleau's understanding of the Chinese concept of filial piety when his mentor sent a fellow Jesuit to be with his mother, whom he would not see for the next seven years.

Father Rouleau was the single most important person in Father Wong's life. He was his guide and mentor, spiritual father and elder brother. He was a luminary model providing an encouraging presence without pushing, projecting, or imposing. Even at their first meeting, Father Rouleau took the young man's looking at his watch as a sign of his need to leave, and later he listened sympathetically as the future Jesuit told him, almost as a confession, of his confusion in thinking about, writing to, and telephoning Gladys Wei so frequently. The relationship was one of trust, and the older man, aware that all things work together for the good for those who love the Lord and are called according to his purpose (Romans 8:28) and that in time of quiet the soul uses its own natural powers freely and tranquilly (*SpEx* 177), advised the younger: "You will know what to do. Simply live accordingly."

And yet Father Rouleau was not inactive or passive. The very first letter of George Wong, who could not get the youthful priest out of his mind, reached Father Rouleau in Nanking. In the midst of bombing and utter chaos, horribly fatiguing work and devastating events, and the disappointment of not being able to carry out the mission of setting up a university center, Father Rouleau answered the letter, graciously revealing his faith, the hope that faith brings, and the love that connects all people. It was the beginning of a deep and lasting bond characterized by a copious correspondence remarkable in its affectionate language, the same kind of language that marks Father Wong's correspondence with me a generation later.

Suffering from exhaustion and a weak heart, Father Rouleau was recuperating in St. Joseph's infirmary when George Wong announced his vocation along with its obstacles. The Jesuit missionary did not hesitate to outline and implement a plan to overcome the obstacles, sponsoring his application to the Novitiate in California and appealing for funds to the readers of *Jesuit Missions* magazine. The two men made a pact like that of Jonathan and David centuries before, becoming soul mates as Confucian elder and younger brothers, their love for each other flowing from their love for God. Patching things up between Gladys and George, whom he called Bernard, Father Rouleau appeared frequently at Aurora University to keep the student encouraged.

Decades later Father Wong would tell me, "Knowing that I belonged to Christ, then and always, I was able to bare my soul's secrets to Father Frank, whose spiritual direction, marked with discernment and kindness, kept me encouraged." This kind of intimacy of brothers in Christ was not characterized by the banter so often evident in Western relationships between men, but it was full of joy and humor and even gentle exhortations as when the elder told the younger, who had complained of the primitive conditions of Yangchow, that he ought to think less about his carcass and more about his spiritual life. In a letter, the scholastic wrote freely about his admiration for Father Farmer without fear of arousing the jealousy of Father Rouleau.

Separated by war and later by Communism, the two would remain spiritually connected in a mentoring relationship that did not put restrictions on the development of the younger or pose threats to the elder. Father Rouleau did not insist that the younger Jesuit follow his footsteps toward the same level of scholarship or toward the same level of activity. He was pleased that George was a natural teacher and overwhelmed with emotion when the Chinese Jesuit returned joyfully to the *laogai* camp in 1981. That Father Rouleau did not attempt to shape his protégé illustrates the classical Chinese character of love in which the sage spares the younger so that he may become himself. Lao-tzu puts it this way:

> And when your constant virtue is complete,
> You'll return to the state of uncarved wood.
> When uncarved wood is cut up, it's turned into vessels;
> When the Sage is used, he becomes the Head of Officials.
> Truly, great carving is done without splitting up.[19]

The translator of this verse informs us that the Sage is someone who will govern (carve) without destroying (splitting up) what is genuine and natural in people.[20] In this case, the relationship of the sage and the pupil closely mirrored the charity or *agape* that St. Paul contrasts with the puffed-up affection (1 Corinthians 13) that might exist in a mentoring relationship gone awry. That Father Wong always closes his conversations with me with an expression of *agape* is a deeply felt emotion binding us to Father Rouleau, in whom he saw Christ Incarnate, and ultimately uniting us with the Father in heaven.

Some ladies, who introduced themselves as Jesuit mothers at a Christmas celebration of the California Jesuit Missionaries, inquired about my relationship to the missionaries. "Oh," I blurted out, "I'm a Jesuit daughter." And that is a good way to describe my relationship with Father Wong although our roles can be rather fluid. On one occasion Father Wong brought up the pope's concerns about Jesuit obedience; quick to take the bait, I argued the other side of the issue. The next morning, Father delivered not so much a homily as a sermon on obedience. On another occasion, he brought up the question of women priests, stating the pope's infallible position that people would not be able to recognize Christ in women as priests. Moreover, he went on, ordaining women risked bringing about a schism in the church. Again, I jumped at the opportunity to discuss the issue and predicted that one day there would be women priests.

"You say that because you want to be a priest," he retorted. But I told him no, that I was simply making a prediction. With that, he said that perhaps I was a prophet, and a few days later he sent me a copy of an article about Juana, the only woman to be admitted into the Society of Jesus. Although the story of Juana is wrought with issues and complications, Father Wong ignored them and focused instead on the favorable points that he wanted to share. A few years later, as we sat in my kitchen talking about the qualities of the archetype priest, he caught me totally off guard. "If there were women priests, you could be one," he volunteered. His own experience did not support the belief that people would not recognize Christ in women priests, and yet he would hold to the white being black if the hierarchical church said it were so (*SpEx* 365), just as the Confucian minister would surrender individual opinion in deference to his prince. This is not about blind obedience; it is about understanding and appreciating the smallness of the individual's experience against the hugeness of the Rock upon which the Holy Spirit whispers like a gentle breeze. We saw this harmonious image repeated over and over again on many walls during our visit to the aforementioned Chinese art exhibit.

As a Chinese Jesuit who witnessed the reversal of the papal injunction against ancestral rites in 1939, Father Wong is keenly aware that mistakes are made on an institutional level. In the case of the Chinese Rites Controversy, he suggested that the eighteenth-century Jesuit missionaries in China should bear some of the responsibility for the edict, since they were slow to respond to requests from Rome for more information. Emerging from prison after Vatican II, he found that the church had changed in a major way, but he was not distressed. His life is not based on ideology but on service to God.

Upon hearing that he had spent the night in a former church on his way to the *laogai* camp, I asked him how he felt; I expected him to share my indignation. But he only smiled and gently replied, "Oh, yes, I took some consolation in the thought that Our Lord had once lived in the tabernacle of this church." And he went about the business of his own examen that evening, asking the Lord to be with him and shed light on his personal mistakes and help him cultivate virtue. Conscious of what he calls his defects—like not being tolerant of his elder sister's sugary love when he was a boy of twelve, being tongue-tied in oratory class, not performing sufficiently at his theology oral examination, lagging behind in the rice paddies—he makes no excuses. Generosity, what Father Provincial was speaking of the night that Father Wong entered the Society of Jesus, starts with himself. Unlike the hyperreligious Pharisees or the hyperhonest villager described by Mencius as the enemy of virtue,[21] he acknowledges his own faults and lacunae and seeks God's grace to grow as he generously forgives others, even the interrogators with their questions, the guards with their guns, and the fallen-away priest who stepped on the crucifix.

Father Wong's prayer life includes the Suscipe and the Examen, of course, but not to the exclusion of other prayers. The delight he shows in a child's smile and in the work of a street artist reflects a spontaneous prayer of thanksgiving. At a concert, Father was moved to appreciative tears by the sacred music of a teenage composer, and I was reminded of one of his Chinese stories. It seems that a peasant was visiting a relative in the city who served him tea made with a precious water. The peasant enjoyed the tea so much that he repeated over and over how excellent it was. The relative, seeing that the guest appreciated fine things, asked if he was referring to the excellence of the tea or of the water. The peasant answered that it was the hotness of the tea that pleased him most. At the concert, it was not the music so much as the enthusiasm of the young musician that touched his heart. Early in the Spiritual Exercises, Ignatius suggests recalling the theme of the next day's prayer upon retiring and then giving full attention to that prayer upon rising the next day, even while dressing (*SpEx* 74). With a lifetime of practice, it is natural that the prayer theme offer itself in the present moment. The newly baptized George Wong simply heard his Buddhist mother tell him, "You can pray while you are walking."

She might have said that he could pray while he was laughing. Father Wong and I both like to laugh; we tend toward laughter. As I was driving one day with a coffee cup in my hand, he offered to take the cup. I told him that I could manage and that he could say his rosary. That reminded him of two confrères who went off the road into a ditch when they tried to combine saying the rosary with driving. We laughed heartily but did not go into a ditch. Another time he was staying at Xavier Hall at the University of San Francisco but did not have the key to get inside after hours. Fortunately, another priest was using his key at the main entrance. I exclaimed, "Quick, Father, follow him," as I shoved him through the door before it closed. Now we laugh about how I got him into the dorm after curfew. In Mexico, we laughed about how the ringing telephone sounded like a grasshopper. There have even been times when, just looking at each other, we were aware that we had had the same thought, and so we simply laughed because no words were necessary.

Although we are comfortable together in silence, our conversations can be rather lively and dynamic as we make rapid connections to various topics, meandering here and there and back again. It has been suggested that Father Wong told me his story because I am a good listener. Recently, however, it dawned on me that the story unfolded not because I am a good listener but rather because I am a good talker. Father Wong's relationship with God is also a conversation, purposeful and yet without agenda, goal, or expected outcome. All Father Wong does is to be who he is and to let God be God in a universe where the moon is not split, where the wave behind affects the wave in front, and where Christ is wholly present in the broken bread and even in the broken body of his imperfect, pilgrim church.

⁜ acknowledgments ⁜

The writing of this story began when I was introduced to Father Wong by Brother Lawrence Thoo of the Jesuit Retreat House in Los Altos, California. The sources for the narrative itself, which I chose to write in the first person, are the conversations between Father Wong and me, some recorded and others not, as well as letters, articles, and meetings with people listed below. The commentary, interspersed throughout the narrative in order to provide contextual information, represents a synthesis of the historical research of scholars, living (Madsen, Myers, Rule, et al.) and dead (e.g., Dunne, Fleming, Ladany), as well as accounts of personal experiences of several people, living (Chu, Kung, and McGlaschan) and dead (Clifford, Phillips, Rouleau, and Tang). The comments on Andreotti of Italy were drawn from Robb's book on the Mafia.

My greatest debt in terms of historical information is to the late Peter Joseph Fleming, S.J., whose monumental work, a dissertation entitled "Chosen for China: The California Province Jesuits in China, 1928–1957: A Case Study in Mission and Culture," was completed in

1987. Consuming more than seven hundred pages, his dissertation is the result of years of reviewing records on mission history, reading issues of *Jesuit Missions* that spanned three decades, uncovering magazine and newspaper articles both popular and esoteric, delving into the documents on the Chinese Rites Controversy, and interviewing the principals. The opus is dedicated to several Jesuits, one of them being Father Wong of whom Fleming wrote on page 479:

> One Jesuit from China who entered the California Province for the China mission and received the first seven years of his training in California and Washington remained in China [after the Communist takeover]. Like the other scholastics who had tickets to leave China, he was told to stay by Jesuit General Jean-Baptiste Janssens. He is sixty-eight-year-old George Bernard Wong (Huang Huachuang), forty-seven years a Jesuit, who was imprisoned for several years, released, and who now teaches English and American studies at Shanghai University. His chapter, however, in "Chosen for China" still remains to be written, a chapter which still remains some years in the writing thereof.

That was the task that I took on. Writing about someone who spent many years of his life in prison might appear to be a somber undertaking, but it was, in fact, a happy experience. One of the main delights was meeting people, new friends who eagerly related facts and impressions about the missionaries in China, the Communist takeover, *laogai* (reform through labor), and the church in China. While one important contributor asked to remain anonymous, it is appropriate to mention others by name. I am especially grateful to Sister Bertille Prus, S.S.S., who, meeting with me in San Francisco, shared her memories of Gladys Wei (Sister Candida in religious life). Having sailed with Father Wong and Sister Candida from San Francisco to Shanghai in 1946, M. Nona McGlashan of Auburn, California, recalled as we chatted over the telephone, the voyage and her experiences in precommunist China. Father Wong, at my side during one of these animated conversations, participated with great enthusiasm as the names of people who had become familiar to me, such as Father Laszio Ladany, were brought up and stories were traded.

Betty Crighton Lee, first at Father Wong's birthday party and later from her sickbed in New York during a speakerphone conversation with Father Wong and me, provided details about life at Christ the King Church in Shanghai, where she first knew the Chinese priest when he was assistant pastor following his ordination in 1951. Their paths would cross again in difficult times and in good times. Sadly, she died of cancer in 1997 before seeing the fruits of our labor.

The accounts given by Sister Mary Celeste Rouleau, R.S.M., about her uncle Father Francis Rouleau, as well as her recollections of the young dandy who arrived in California to begin his novitiate in 1939, enlivened the unfolding of the story; Sister Celeste also furnished some of the photographs included here. Ellen and Henry Yang sent the snapshots taken at Father Wong's eightieth birthday party, and Father Wong's nephew Eddie Huang shared the family album with me. Father James Chevedden, S.J., put me in touch with Father Barry Martinson, S.J., in Taiwan who, in turn, found more photographs. Mary and John Liu invited me to join them and their friends and relatives at a dinner at which they honored the beloved teacher while educating me about chopsticks. Invited to lunch, along with three companions from my Ignatian retreat of 1995, by Father Efrem Trettel, O.F.M., of San Francisco, I spoke of Father Wong only to learn of Father Trettel's experiences in China as a missionary from Italy.

Responses to my questions sent via e-mail about Ignatian and missionary history and about current scientific dialogue between the Jesuits and the Chinese were returned respectively by Dr. Paul Rule of La Trobe University in Australia; Father Dick Vande Velde, S.J., of Loyola University in Chicago; Brother Peter Pontolillo, S.M., secretary general of the Marianist order in Rome; and Father George V. Coyne, S.J., of the Vatican Observatory. In fact, Dr. Rule spent a great deal of time reviewing the draft, providing his insights and corrections. My e-mail query to the Laogai Foundation in an attempt to gain information about the school Harry Wu attended as a child in Shanghai prompted a telephone call from Harry Wu himself, who insisted on meeting Father Wong that very day. The two of us ended up joining Father Wong and Father Paul Bernadicou for dinner that evening at the Sacred Heart Jesuit Center in Los Gatos.

I would also like to thank Mark Mir, research fellow and archivist, at the Ricci Institute for Chinese-Western Cultural History at the University of San Francisco. I appreciate his help in finding materials, in providing an excellent work environment, and in making information available to scholars throughout the world via the Internet. I am grateful to Dr. Xiaoxin Wu, current director of the Ricci Institute, to May Lee, also of the Ricci Institute, and to Father Raymond Woo, S.J., for their help with Chinese words. Another important contribution was the careful proofreading provided by Linda Brogden, a valued friend from Hewlett-Packard to whom I felt comfortable entrusting this project. Lou Sniderman, also a dear friend from Hewlett-Packard, assisted in scanning the photographs and touching them up for my digital files. There was one of Father Rouleau and young Wong at Zikawei, from an old copy of *Jesuit Missions* pulled out of the storage bins at Gleeson Library at the University of San Francisco, that was in particularly poor shape before treatment by Lou's electronic paintbrush. I would also like to thank my manager, Michael Kalashian, along with Erin Hickey and Audrey McGowan for their support.

I am also grateful to the pastor, Father Jerome Foley, and the entire community of St. Thomas More Church in San Francisco; to my parents, Naomi and Arthur Young; to my son, Christian Devaux; to my very good friends Renate Otterbach and Josefina and Miguel Madrigal; and especially to my husband, Ronald Larson. A software engineer for Hewlett-Packard, Ron has spent his free time cooking for us, taking messages, videotaping Father Wong at Mass in Mexico, sharing the sunset at Puerto Vallarta with us, and mostly just being present, as he quietly observes, "Father Wong is a man totally free of bitterness."

The important suggestion of Dr. Emile Wilson, formerly of the University of San Francisco, to rely on reflection and meditation was a blessing, and so were the hermeneutic principles of Father Vernon Ruland for exploring religious truths and of Father Daniel Kendall for examining texts. Father Denis Collins has also been a guide from the very start of this journey. Along with the suggestions that he penned in the margins of the draft was the welcome comment about its having been his spiritual reading for the summer of 1997. The credit for making this reading available to a broader audience goes to Linda Schlafer of Loyola Press. Her skills as an editor are complemented by a generous sensitivity and collaborative spirit that have made this undertaking a pleasant work experience.

Father Edward Malatesta graciously enlightened me on the topic of the church in China, directing me to appropriate literature. With great generosity, Father Malatesta, in spite of his demanding schedule of retreat direction on top of his work as director of the Ricci Institute for Chinese-Western Cultural History at the University of San Francisco, meticulously reviewed the entire dissertation, returning it to me with comments, corrections, and truly helpful suggestions. The fact that Father Malatesta was well acquainted with Father Wong made his insight especially meaningful. His sudden death in January 1998 represents a major loss to the Ricci Institute; his scholarly contribution to the growing understanding about spiritual matters in the East and the West must be continued so that his vision of the encounter between Christianity and the Chinese culture may be more fully realized. Fortunately, Father Malatesta was able to see this document on the life of a twentieth-century Chinese Jesuit come to fruition.

Most of all, I thank Father Paul Bernadicou for walking through the entire process with Father Wong and me. Supportive of the plan for Father Wong to accompany my husband and me to Puerto

Vallarta, Mexico, so that we could record our conversations at leisure, he joined Father Malatesta in reviewing the original transcripts in their very rough form. Even while on sabbatical, Father Bernadicou read and reread drafts that came to him in Cambridge, in London, and in Paris via Federal Express and fax, sometimes spending long hours on the telephone or in meetings with me or simply calling to offer a word of encouragement. Never once did he complain that he had already read one draft or that he was too busy or too weary. Father Bernadicou's organizational skills and personal strength certainly contribute to his capacity to manufacture time and transmit energy, but it is obvious that there is another Source for these miracles. In different ways, Fathers Wong and Bernadicou represent Eastern and Western love and wisdom, *agape,* and *gnosis;* it is natural to call them *Rabbi* or *Teacher.*

Claudia Devaux
San Francisco, July 31, 1999
Feast of St. Ignatius of Loyola

✣ endnotes ✣

1. This quotation is from remarks made by Fr. Malatesta at a doctoral defense.

2. Wei-ming Tu, "The Confucian Perception of Adulthood," in *Adulthood,* edited by Erik H. Erikson (New York: W. W. Norton and Company, 1978), 125.

3. Wing-tsit Chan, "The Individual in Chinese Religions," in *The Status of the Individual in the East and West,* edited by Charles A. Moore (Honolulu: University of Hawaii Press, 1968), 190.

4. P. Dudon, S.J., *St. Ignatius of Loyola* (Milwaukee: Bruce, 1949), 292.

5. Wing-tsit Chan, "The Individual in Chinese Religions," 191.

6. Ibid., 188, quoting The Great Learning, an ancient Chinese text.

7. Huston Smith, *Forgotten Truth: The Common Vision of the World's Religions* (1976; reprint, San Francisco: HarperSanFrancisco, 1992), 149–150.

8. C. S. Lewis, *The Four Loves* (1960, reprint New York: Harcourt, Brace and Company, 1988), 131.

9. Dom Aelred Graham, *Zen Catholicism: A Suggestion* (New York: Harcourt, Brace and World, 1963), 42.

10. Ibid., 47.

11. Joseph Joubert, *Pensées* (Paris: Perrin et Cie., 1922), 101.

12. Lao-tzu, *Lao-tzu Tao-te Ching: A New Translation Based on the Recently Discovered Ma-wang-tui Texts*, 59 and 80.

13. Wei-ming Tu, "The Confucian Perception of Adulthood," 114.

14. Ibid., 124.

15. Ibid., 120–121.

16. Wing-tsit Chan, "The Individual in Chinese Religions," 191, 193.

17. Ibid., 193.

18. Graham, *Zen Catholicism*, 151.

19. Lao-tzu, *Tao-te Ching: A New Translation*, 80.

20. Ibid., 242.

21. Wei-ming Tu, "The Confucian Perception of Adulthood," 115.

❖ bibliography ❖

Books and Dissertations

Becker, Kurt, S.J. *I Met a Traveler: The Triumph of Father Phillips.* New York: Farrar, Straus, and Company, 1958.

Butcher, Beverly Joan. "Remembrance, Emulation, Imagination: The Chinese and Chinese American Catholic Ancestor Memorial Service." Ph.D. diss., University of Michigan, 1994.

Butterfield, Fox. *China: Alive in the Bitter Sea.* New York: Times Books, 1982.

The Catholic Church in Modern China. Edited by Edmond Tang and Jean-Paul Wiest. Maryknoll, New York: Orbis Books, 1993.

Chan, Kim-kwong. "Towards a Contextual Ecclesiology: The Catholic Church in the People's Republic of China (1979–1983): Its Life and Theological Implications." Ph.D. diss., St. Paul University, 1987.

Chinese Rites Controversy: Its History and Meaning. Edited by D. E. Mungello. Jointly published by Institut Monumenta Serica, Sankt Augustin, and the Ricci Institute for Chinese-Western Cultural History, San Francisco, 1994.

Clifford, John W., S.J. *In the Presence of My Enemies.* New York: W. W. Norton and Company, Inc., 1963.

Cowell, Ralph A. *Confucius, the Buddha, and Christ: A History of the Gospel in Chinese*. Maryknoll, New York: Orbis Books, 1986.

Documents of the Thirty-first and Thirty-second General Congregations of the Society of Jesus. Edited by John W. Padberg, S.J. St. Louis: The Institute of Jesuit Sources, 1977.

Documents of the Thirty-fourth General Congregation of the Society of Jesus. Edited by John McCarthy, S.J. St. Louis: The Institute of Jesuit Sources, 1995.

Dudon, P., S.J. *St. Ignatius of Loyola*. Milwaukee: Bruce, 1949.

Dunne, George H., S.J. *A Generation of Giants: The Story of the Jesuits in China in the Last Decade of the Ming Dynasty*. Notre Dame, Ind.: University of Notre Dame Press, 1962.

Fleming, David L., S.J. *The Spiritual Exercises of St. Ignatius: A Literal Translation and a Contemporary Reading*. St. Louis: The Institute of Jesuit Sources, 1991.

Fleming, Peter Joseph, S.J. "Chosen for China: The California Province Jesuits in China, 1928–1957: A Case Study in Mission and Culture." Ph.D. diss., Graduate Theological Union, Berkeley, Calif., 1987.

Graham, Dom Aelred. *Zen Catholicism: A Suggestion*. New York: Harcourt, Brace & World, 1963.

Hinton, William. *Fashen: A Documentary of Revolution in a Chinese Village*. New York: Random House, 1966.

Ignatius of Loyola: The Spiritual Exercises and Selected Works. Edited by George E. Ganss, S.J. New York: Paulist Press, 1991.

Joubert, Joseph. *Pensées*. Paris: Perrin et Cie., 1922.

Kristof, Nicholas D., and Sheryl Wudunn. *China Wakes: The Struggle for the Soul of a Rising Power*. New York: Vintage Books, 1995.

Ladany, Laszlo, S.J. *The Catholic Church in China*. New York: Freedom House, 1987.

_____. *The Communist Party of China and Marxism*. Stanford, Calif.: Stanford University Press, 1988.

Lao-tzu. *Tao te Ching*. Translated by Gia-fu Feng and Jane English. Mount Shasta, Calif.: Earth Heart, 1972.

_____. *Te-tao Ching: A New Translation Based on the Recently Discovered Ma-wang-tui Texts*. Translated by Robert G. Hendricks. New York: Ballantine Books, 1989.

Lazzarato, Angelo S. *The Catholic Church in Post-Mao China*. Hong Kong: Holy Spirit Centre, 1982.

Lewis, C. S. *The Four Loves*. 1960. Reprint, New York: Harcourt, Brace & Company, 1988.

MacInnis, Donald E. *Religion in China Today: Policy and Practice*. Maryknoll, New York: Orbis Books, 1989.

Madsen, Richard. *China's Catholics: Tragedy and Hope in an Emerging Civil Society*. Berkeley, Calif.: University of California Press, 1998.

Martin, Mary Lou, M.M., and Donald MacInnis. *Values and Religion in China Today*. Maryknoll, New York: Maryknoll Fathers, 1985.

Martinson, Barry, S.J. *Celestial Dragon: A Life and Selected Writings of Fr. Francis Rouleau*. Taipei: Taipei Ricci Institute, 1998.

McGlashan, M. Nona. *O Days of Wind and Moon*. Santa Barbara, Calif.: Fithian Press, 1997.

Meissner, W. W., S.J., M.D. *Ignatius of Loyola: The Psychology of a Saint*. New Haven, Conn.: Yale University Press, 1992.

Minamiki, George, S.J. *The Chinese Rites Controversy from Its Beginnings to Modern Times*. Chicago: Loyola University Press, 1985.

Monsterleet, Jean, S.J. *Martyrs in China*. Translated by Antonia Pakenham. Chicago: Henry Regnery Company, 1953.

Mungello, D. E. *Curious Land: Jesuit Accommodation and the Origins of Sinolog*. Paperback edition. Honolulu: University of Hawaii Press, 1989.

Myers, James T. *Enemies without Guns: The Catholic Church in China*. New York: Paragon House, 1991.

O'Malley, William J., S.J. *The Fifth Week*. Chicago: Loyola University Press, 1976.

One Hundred Roman Documents concerning the Chinese Rites Controversy (1645–1941). Translated by Donald F. St. Sure, S.J. Edited by Ray R. Noll. San Francisco: Ricci Institute for Chinese-Western Cultural History, 1992.

Palmer, Gretta. *God's Underground in Asia.* New York: Appleton-Century-Crofts, Inc., 1953.

Ricci, Matteo, S.J. *The True Meaning of the Lord of Heaven.* Translated by Douglas Lancashire and Peter Ho Kuo-chen. Edited by Edward J. Malatesta, S.J. St. Louis: The Institute of Jesuit Sources, 1985.

Robb, Peter. *Midnight in Sicily: On Art, Food, History, Travel, and La Cosa Nostra.* Boston: Faber and Faber, 1996.

Rule, Paul A. *Kung-tzu or Confucius? The Jesuit Interpretation of Confucianism.* Sydney: Allen and Unwin, 1986.

Smith, Huston. *Forgotten Truth: The Common Vision of the World's Religion.* 1976. Reprint. San Francisco: HarperSanFrancisco, 1992.

Stockwell, Francis Olin. *With God in Red China: The Story of Two Years in Chinese Communist Prisons.* New York: Harper and Brothers, 1953.

Sun-Childers, Jaia, and Douglas Childers. *The White-Haired Girl: Bittersweet Adventures of a Little Red Soldier.* New York: Picador, 1996.

Tang, Dominic, S.J. *How Inscrutable His Ways! Memoirs.* 3rd ed. Hong Kong: Condor Production Limited, 1994.

Trettel, Efrem, O.F.M. *Rivers-Rice Fields-Souls.* Translated by Elsa Micallef. Chicago: Franciscan Press, 1965.

Wu, Harry, and Carolyn Wakeman. *Bitter Winds.* New York: John Wiley and Sons, 1994.

Wu, Harry, and George Vecsey. *Troublemaker: One Man's Crusade against China's Cruelty.* New York: Random House, 1996.

Articles, Essays, and Booklets

Aschenbrenner, George. *Review for Religious* 31 (1972).

Anderson, George M., S.J. "Jesuits in Jail: Ignatius to the Present." *Studies in the Spirituality of the Jesuits* 27, no. 4 (September 1995).

Chan, Wing-tsit. "The Individual in Chinese Religions." In *The Status of the Individual in the East and West.* Edited by Charles A. Moore. Honolulu: University of Hawaii Press, 1968.

China Pilgrim. "Sino-Vatican Reconciliation and Chinese Characteristics." Translated by Betty Ann Macheu. In *Tripod* 16, no. 95 (September–October 1996).

Ching, Julia. "Hyphenated Christianity." *China Notes* 16, no. 3 (summer 1978). In Ralph A. Cowell. *Confucius, the Buddha, and Christ: A History of the Gospel in Chinese.* Maryknoll, New York: Orbis Books, 1986.

Chu, Margaret. "A Catholic Girl in Prison in China." In James T. Myers. *Enemies without Guns: The Catholic Church in China.* New York: Paragon House, 1991.

Dunne, George H., S.J. "The Church in China." *The Tablet,* 23 February 1980.

Funk, Mary Margaret, O.S.B. "Journey to the Roof of the World." *America,* 3 August 1996.

Gernet, Jacques. "Chine et christianisme." In *Action et réaction.* Paris, 1982. In David E. Mungello. *Curious Land: Jesuit Accommodation and the Origins of Sinology.* Paperback edition. Honolulu: University of Hawaii Press, 1989.

Madsen, Richard. "China's Catholics: Devout and Divided." *Commonweal,* 25 April 1997.

O'Hare, Joseph A., S.J. "Of Many Things." (Editorial on the interfaith service at St. Patrick's Cathedral on the occasion of the Dalai Lama's visit.) *America,* 22 September 1979, page ii.

Rouleau, Francis A., S.J., "Back on the Farm: The Odyssey of George Bernard Wong (Huang)." *[Jesuit] California Province News,* February 1982.

_____. "China Had the First Auto." *Jesuit Missions* 21 (November 1947), 241–243.

_____. "Chinese Rites Controversy" in *New Catholic Encyclopedia,* vol. 3. New York: McGraw Hill, 1967, 611.

_____. "From a Nanking Cellar." *Jesuit Missions* 12 (January 1938), 6–7.

_____. "The Homesick Millions in Shanghai." *Jesuit Missions* 14 (December 1940), 32–33, 55.

_____. "They're Bombing Our Train." *Jesuit Missions* 13 (January 1939), 10–11, 28.

_____. "Wake Up and Be Buddha." *Jesuit Missions* 15 (May 1941), 126–127, 139–140.

_____. "Wedding Bells in Old Cathay." *Jesuit Missions* 12 (January 1938), 290–292.

Shelton, Charles M., S.J. "Friendship in Jesuit Life: The Joys, the Struggles, the Possibilities." *Studies in the Spirituality of the Jesuits* 27, no. 5 (November 1995).

Tam, Patrick. Letter to the *National Catholic Reporter,* 8 November 1996.

Tao, Cecilia. "Healing the Conflict in the Chinese Catholic Church." *America,* 17 August 1996.

Tu, Wei-ming. "The Confucian Perception of Adulthood." In *Adulthood.* Edited by Erik H. Erikson. New York: W. W. Norton and Company, 1978.

White, Mark. "Matteo Ricci's Lesson to a Modern Missionary." *America,* 17 August 1996.

Williams, S. Wells. *The Middle Kingdom.* 2nd ed. Revised. New York, 1883. In *Chinese Rites Controversy: Its History and Meaning.* Edited by D. E. Mungello. Jointly published by Institut Monumenta Serica, Sankt Augustin, and the Ricci Institute for Chinese-Western Cultural History, San Francisco, 1994.

Wong, George B., S.J., pseud. Bernard Brown. "Candle in the Wind: A Prisoner's Testimony." *The Tablet* 24, no. 31 (December 1994).

_____. "China's Violent Minority." *Jesuit Missions* 19 (July–August 1945) 158–159.

_____. "Double Seventh." *Jesuit Missions* 18 (October 1944) 238–239.

_____. "Red Star over China." *Jesuit Missions* 19 (January–February 1945) 7.

_____. "There's a Little Quiet in China." *Jesuit Missions* 21 (January 1947), 116–117.

✤ permissions ✤

ALSO AVAILABLE FROM LOYOLA PRESS...

Celestial Dragon: A Life and Selected Writings of Fr. Francis Rouleau
from Barry Martinson, S.J.

> Since returning to China I have been absorbed in my teaching work here at the scholasticate. I am glad to be back with my adopted people and to be working for them. In some ways, it is easier to follow Our Lord here than at home: we are very poor, for one thing . . . much poorer than I found things in Europe. But no one, I am sure, complains; and our sacrifices are offered up for the conversion of these dear people. Conditions are getting worse and worse: communism is advancing, and wherever this ruthless steamroller goes it crushes out the church. In the big coastal cities there are thousands of refugee priests and sisters driven out of their missions by the Communists. The stories of persecution and destruction are heartrending. But . . . confidence in Divine Providence! He knows how to draw good out of evil. I returned last week from a week's visit with our fathers in our California Mission (Yangchow: about ten hours by train, boat, autobus from here). The Communists are only thirteen miles from this place, the center of our Mission. We are preparing for the worst; but the fathers are all cheerful and truly full of a Christly spirit of sacrifice and zeal. Here in this big coastal city, Shanghai, the situation is much more secure, but there are many who think that sooner or later the Communists will launch a full-scale attack against Shanghai. . . . We are in the hands of God.
>
> *June 11, 1948*
> *Shanghai*

Celestial Dragon: A Life and Selected Writings of Fr. Francis Rouleau
by Barry Martinson, S.J.
$25.00 Hardcover
435 pages
ISBN: 957-9185-53-0

To order this book or receive information on other fine Loyola Press titles, call 1-800-621-1008, fax (773) 281-0555, or visit our Web site at www.loyolapress.org.